SANS SOUCI SPA DINING

SANS SOUCI SPA DINING

FOOD FOR HEALTH AND HAPPINESS

by

Susanne Kircher, RN

Nutritional Analysis
Vital Vitamins
by
Carol Soehner, RD

Art Work
by
Tina Stuart

Edited
by
Shirley Maxwell
Columbus, Ohio

Trudy Knox, Publisher
Granville, Ohio 43023

SANS SOUCI SPA DINING.
Copyright © 1993 by Susanne Kircher
All rights reserved.   Printed in the United States of America.

Trudy Knox, Publisher
168 Wildwood Drive
Granville, OH 43023-1073

First Edition

ISBN: 0-9611354-8-4
LCN: 93-78351

To my parents who gave me life and love

To my husband who believes in me and gives me support

To YOU, the reader of this book,
in your quest for Health and Happiness

Heartfelt thanks go to:

Patty Davidson, manager/chef
Alice Breece, dietitian
Marcia Holmes, fitness director
Betty McKay, friend and mentor
Jeneene Brengelman, Ph.D., consultant
Marsha O'Shaughnessy, public affairs specialist

v

CONTENTS

SANS SOUCI SPA LIFE

FOREWORD

Good health and body fitness are a way of life at Sans Souci. Guests learn new ways of taking care of themselves with exercise, relaxation and wholesome food. As this combination enhances love of self, it is apparent that providing wholesome food tastefully served is the application of good nutrition with love.

Susie Kircher, director of Sans Souci, is aware of the importance of food prepared to appeal to all of the senses. Her food plan includes lots of color for eye appeal, taste sensations, pleasing aromas and delightful contrasts in textures - soft and crisp, hot and cold. Food is always so attractively arranged and served that guests feel truly cared for and cherished.

This recipe collection illustrates how food can be prepared and served with love. Susie applies principles of good, wholesome nutrition and prepares her dishes with a creative flair, using seasonings of herbs and spices. These recipes are a new adventure in eating enjoyment and health power. Every health-concerned person who wants to build new vitality into her or his life will treasure *Sans Souci Spa Dining*.

Guests leave Sans Souci with the skills, motivation and the knowledge to make needed changes for a more healthy life style. Every health oriented person desiring to add a new dimension to their food preparation skills will find this book a real treasure.

ALICE BREECE, Ph.D.

Licensed Dietitian and Nutrition Consultant
Lecturer, Sans Souci

INTRODUCTION

"I can eat that much food and still lose weight?"

"Even my children will like tuna burgers and fatfree onion rings. How can I do them at home?"

"If healthy living feels so good, I'm sold on it."

During my fourteen years at Sans Souci, comments like these echoed through the Spa. They inspired me to write this book. My goal is to help you acquire habits of healthy living that you can practice at home.

Along with the 18-Point Health Plan you will find recipes that are simple and require little preparation time. They pack the most nutrients into as few calories as possible. Fresh foods, herbs and spices combine into mouth-watering new taste delights. You'll never miss the fat.

Guests and Sans Souci staff members provided ideas for many of the recipes. I also retrieved some from the memory of my European background, recreating my mother's and grand-mother's favorites. Others are derived from established recipes that I modified to suit the need for a health-conscious life.

Yes, you can live without the salty, sugary, greasy taste of "normal" food. Taste buds change when you give them a chance.

When I first introduced my family to spa cuisine, I was in for quite a challenge. At the dining room table while reaching for dressing, our youngest son Andy asked, "Is this the healthy stuff or the good stuff?" Some time later I knew that I had gained a convert when he looked through our refrigerator asking me, "Do we still have some homemade dressing and Spa Musli?"

Experience for yourself how wonderful the right combination of natural "life-giving" foods can taste. This book is for people who enjoy eating and intend to live a long, healthy and happy life. It is dedicated to you and to your health.

> Walk for fitness
> Eat for health
> Nourish the spirit
> Empower your life

CHAPTER 1
THE SANS SOUCI
18-POINT HEALTH PLAN

*Only if we lose it
do we know the value of health*

The first 28 years of my life were a struggle against disease and overweight. I continued to ignore warning signs until I developed a recurrent kidney infection which sapped my energy and threatened my life. It was at that time that a friend of mine handed me a book on healing written by a Swedish doctor, Are Wareland.

He recommended to eat 80% of all food in the form of raw or slightly steamed vegetables, fruits, soaked seeds and grains. I was desperate enough to try it.

This brought my addiction to sugary cakes and meat to a screeching halt. To me it was like a miracle that not only my kidney infection disappeared but I also lost weight and felt an abundance of energy. The pull of my old habits was strong. I slipped back several times, only to find myself again suscepti- ble to infections and weight gain. Now I am sold on treating myself right and making healthy choices. One of my new decisions was to create a life-enhancing work environment where, as a nurse, I could help others.

When I mentioned to my husband that I wanted to open a resort for health and weight control, he replied, "Why go through all that trouble? Just tell people to eat less and exer- cise more." First I laughed at his remark but soon recognized that he, as a naturally thin person, didn't realize the struggle that many people have with weight control. Now he, too, is convinced that there are people who need help with this problem.

Some gain fat easily, and some remain skinny no matter how much they eat or how little they exercise. Some of us are overly proficient at storing fat and more reluctant at burning it. Obesity can be a vicious cycle. The more fat that is stored, the easier it becomes to store fat and the more difficult it is to exercise.

The way out of the yo-yo cycle began for me when I stopped focusing on pounds and started to focus on develop- ing a healthy body. The 18-Point Health Plan is simple. And like most good things in life, it is easy to remember. It was my ticket to a fit and healthy life. I am confident you, too, can make it work.

The number 18 symbolizes life and vitality. It is not a coincidence that our European parcourse has 18 exercise stations.

- 18 miles of walking a week
- 18% of total calories from fat
- 18 x 2 = 36 grams of fiber a day
- 18 hugs a week

18 Miles of Walking a Week

A mountain is climbed one step at a time

While working at an international sports resort, I provided medical first aid to the Rumanian Olympic sports teams. The high motivation level of the team members fascinated me. When an injury occurred during training and I ordered "R I C E = Rest, Ice, Compression, Elevation," each team member invented creative ways to stay fit. They did not want to violate my order to rest the injured limb, but they would continue to do sit-ups, push-ups, weight lifting in bed or hopping on one leg. Competition was fierce and the psychological and financial rewards for staying on the team were great. So fit they stayed.

Until then, I had many good "reasons" why I couldn't exercise. Soon I discovered that I had the choice between results and reasons. After trying several short cuts, I finally discovered ways to do it, not reasons why I couldn't. I am glad I did!

Now exercise is one of the great joys of my life. I treasure the morning walks with my husband, Konrad. There is no newspaper, TV, phone or doorbell to interrupt our conversations. Yes, we walk in the winter too. Our down-filled parkas help us keep warm in the coldest of winter weather.

As a fat-burning activity, walking is the queen of all exercises. Muscles burn fat only when they are worked continually for an extended period of time. Speed is not as important as duration. It is better to walk for an hour at the lower end of your target heart rate than to run for 15 minutes at an exhausting speed.

To find your recommended target heart rate for aerobic exercise, a general rule of thumb is to take 200 minus your age, minus 10%. For example: If you are 40 years old take 200 minus 40 = 160 minus 16 = 144. The recommended training heart rate in a healthy person at age 40 would be approximately 144 beats per minute, as measured by your pulse rate. Any exercise that involves most of the large muscles for at least 20 minutes at the target heart rate is called aerobic exercise. It's called aerobic because more air/oxygen is used by working the large muscle groups. Besides walking it can be swimming, bicycling, cross-country skiing or jogging.

At the beginning of an aerobic exercise, your body uses stored energy from muscles and liver. Fat-burning kicks in later. Dr. Kenneth Cooper has coined the expression of "L.S.D.- Long Slow Distance-walking" to burn fat.

Reducing calories without exercise does more harm than good. One pound of muscle tissue is lost out of every four pounds of weight you lose without exercise. If you regain it, you regain fat only, thus changing your muscle to fat ratio and lowering your metabolism. This, in turn, makes it harder to lose weight.

With exercise your body builds stronger muscles. Muscles use more calories even at rest, helping you to lose weight. During exercise your metabolic rate will increase and will stay elevated for hours after you have stopped as your "revved up" body returns to normal.

Walking keeps the joints healthy, the muscles and bones strong and the cardiovascular system fit. It is fun, effective, easy, inexpensive and virtually injury-free. All you need is a good pair of shoes, socks, a desire for a trim, fit body and maybe a friend with whom to walk. You can be your own best friend and walk solo.

I have cultivated a set of friendships centered around long walks and talks. Yvonne Dalton came as a guest to Sans Souci, and soon we became friends. Now we both cherish our long walks and talks which always seem too short. Yvonne's view: "During walking in a nature setting it is so much easier to get in touch with feelings. If there is a trusted friend to listen, it can be a real healing process. The benefits are physical, mental and spiritual. Long nature walks bring us closer to God, to ourselves and to our friends." Yvonne, a psychiatrist, tells me that depressed patients do better when exercising regularly. During aerobic exercise the brain releases endorphins, elevating the mood and counteracting depression.

If you are sedentary, check with a doctor before embarking on an exercise program. Find a doctor who likes to exercise and supports you on your path to health and fitness. Start with one-half mile and work yourself slowly up to three miles a day, five to six times a week. It takes several months of training to be able to walk at a brisk pace 18 miles a week. Be gentle with yourself.

When starting out

- drink one glass of water before and after walking
- stretch major muscle groups for five minutes before and after walking
- don't exercise vigorously on a full stomach
- increase both time and intensity of your workout every three weeks by 10% until you reach your desired fitness level and are able to walk briskly four miles at a stretch
- walk at a pace you feel increases your breathing but not to the point you are out of breath. This is called the level of perceived exertion
- swing your arms to increase fitness level. As you advance you may want to consider power walking and interval training. Power walking incorporates exaggerated arm and hip movements and interval training alternates levels of intensity of exercise
- find a walking partner. It's safer, more fun, and you are more likely to stick to your new fitness way of life
- until you do, be your own best friend and walk anyway.

While living in Europe I learned to appreciate and love walking, I still do. In the "old country" everybody who is able walks somewhere; to school, to church, to the store, to nature.

I want to travel as far as I can go
I want to reach the joy that's in my soul
And change the limitations that I know
And feel my mind and spirit grow.

From Champneys Spa in England

18% of Total Calories From Fat

Success is getting up just one more time
than you fall down

Of all the food we eat, fat poses the greatest hazard to our waistlines, health and life expectancy. Jane Brody, in her *Good Food Book* claims, "Fat is our worst nutritional failing."

Average fat consumption in our country today is 38% to 42% of total calories. The American Heart Association recommends that 30% or less of total calories come from fat. My experience supports a fat intake limit of 15% to 18% - for several reasons.

It is more difficult to shed extra pounds and to keep them off with a high fat diet. One gram of fat has nine calories as opposed to carbohydrates or protein which have only four calories per gram. Fats have 2.25 times more calories than carbohydrates. They are mostly empty calories that may easily be stored on hips and waistlines and may clog up arteries.

Feeling satisfied and full after a meal is caused by the amount of food in the stomach, not by the calorie count. Because a small amount of fat has a large amount of calories and no fiber, it is easy to eat far too many fat calories, as in a candy bar, long before the stomach feels full. A large salad and a baked potato with Fitness Cheese can equal one small chocolate bar in calories. A chocolate bar leaves room for two more chocolate bars, while the salad and potato fills you up and provides a balanced meal.

The fat you eat is the fat you wear. Your body is more efficient at converting excess fat you eat into body fat than it is at converting excess carbohydrate or protein into body fat. Even if you do not have to watch your weight, it is still crucial to reduce fat consumption. Almost half of Americans die of heart and vascular diseases. A high fat diet, especially saturated fats, contributes greatly to cardiovascular diseases and cancer.

The major appeal of fat in the diet is its flavor-enhancing property. The good news is that taste buds can be fooled with low fat substitutes. Over and over again guests at Sans Souci praise the Fitness Cheese which has the same creamy consistency as cream cheese. Fitness Cheese has 3% fat while cream cheese is 90% fat. Our delicious 4% fat potato chips receive an A+ rating over the greasy 52% fat commercial potato chips. The Sans Souci Mayo with 3% fat tastes better than regular mayonnaise with its 99% fat content.

When buying prepared foods, place special emphasis on low fat. To find out what percentage of fat calories you get, check the label for the total amount of calories per serving. Next, check how many grams of fat are in one serving. Multiply the total grams of fat by 9. Each gram of fat has 9 calories. Divide that number, calories from fat, by the total number of calories per serving.

The result will show you how high a percentage of total calories actually come from fat. For example, if one serving has 260 calories and there are 17 grams of fat per serving, take 17 times 9 = 153, divided by 260 = 59%. That means that 59% of the total calories come from fat.

Starting in 1994, new food labeling laws will make it easier to check the fat content of products, but you still need to pay attention.

Here is an example of new food labeling pertaining to the fat content in a ½ cup serving of macaroni and cheese.

Calories 260	Calories from fat 120
Total fat 13g	Daily value: 20%
Saturated fat 5g	Daily value: 25%
Cholesterol 30g	Daily value: 10%

Unfortunately, these new food labels do not indicate the most important factor, the percentage of fat from total calories. You will need to figure it out yourself and here is how.

Divide the calories from fat by the total amount of calories per serving. In our example, 120 calories from fat, divided by 260 = total amount of calories = .46 x 100 = 46%. If the above mentioned example of macaroni and cheese would state that it provides 46% of total calories from fat, which it does, we could see its fatty nature at one glance.

Pay attention to those "daily value" numbers. They are misleading because they tell you that this product gives you 20% of your total fat for the day, based on 2,000 calories and 30% fat per day. High? I think so. 2,000 calories per day is too high for most women. 30% fat from total calories is high for both women and men. Why base daily recommended values on 30% fat which by all modern standards is at the high end of an ideal fat/calorie ratio? 15% to 18% of total calories from fat is nutritionally safer and can be obtained with a focus on food choices.

There is no need to fret about getting too little fat. For good nutrition all we need is the equivalent of one tablespoon of vegetable oil a day to supply the essential fatty acids that the body cannot make on its own. We don't need to add processed, concentrated fats or oils to our daily fare. The oil we need can easily be obtained by eating a variety of seeds, grains, legumes and vegetables.

Fat percent by calories of some foods

5% to 18% fat: vegetables, fruits, grains, legumes like beans, peas and lentils, bread, most cereals, skim milk products, Fitness Cheese, seafood like scallops, shrimp, white fish, skinned turkey breast

19% to 30% fat: some fish like cod, oysters, skinned chicken breast, muffins

31% to 40% fat: some fish like flounder or halibut, skinned chicken dark meat, granola, pizza, 2% milk, low fat yogurt

41% to 50% fat: extra lean beef, fried chicken, canned salmon and sardines, whole milk.

51% to 75% fat: most hard cheeses like Swiss, American, Cheddar, eggs, lamb chops, pork lean cuts, veal, ice cream

76% fat and more: bacon, some beef like regular hamburger or untrimmed sirloin, cold cuts, cream, mayonnaise, cream cheese, olives, nuts, pumpkin, sesame, sunflower seeds, avocado

On the light side, fat percent by calories

1%:	potato
5%:	apples, celery, skinned turkey breast
6%:	broccoli, pineapple
9%:	asparagus, cabbage
10%:	strawberries, corn
11%:	green bell pepper
14%:	apples
18%:	chicken breast
19%:	oat bran

On the high side, fat percent by calories

53%	roast beef
55%:	lean pork chops
60%:	Parmesan cheese
66%	sirloin steak, Swiss cheese
69%:	cashews
72%:	peanut butter, salami
74%:	American cheese, bologna, Cheddar cheese
78%:	bacon
85%:	green olives
95%:	whipping cream

FAT FACTS

• Fatfree doesn't mean no fat. Under current labeling laws, food that provides less than half a gram of fat per serving can be called fatfree.

• Margarine isn't lower in fat than butter. Both provide 11 grams of fat and 99 calories per tablespoon. Air whipped margarines provide fewer calories per tablespoon. The softer margarines are lower in saturated fat.

• Ground turkey isn't necessarily lower in fat than ground meat. Most brands have dark meat and skin ground into the mix which can make them just as high in fat as ground beef. The only low fat ground turkey is made with nothing but ground turkey breast.

• Ground beef labeled lean can provide up to 65% of calories from fat.

• 2% milk is not lowfat, as the label states. It provides 38% of total calories from fat. When the label says 2% fat milk, it is referring to the amount of milk fat by weight, not by calories. But what you really want to know is how much fat by calories a food item provides. 1% milk provides 26% of calories from fat. ½% milk provides 10% of calories from fat. Skim milk has only traces of fat. Whole milk provides 50% of total calories from fat.

• Light oils are not lower in fat than regular oils, just lighter in color or flavor.

• Cholesterol-free is often used as a selling gimmick. All cholesterol comes from animal products. Therefore there is no need to label a vegetable or grain product as cholesterol-free. In contrast, lowfat animal products can be high in cholesterol like liver, veal, pork, beef or shrimp. However, it is not so much the cholesterol you consume as the amount of total fats that can raise your blood cholesterol level.

• Carob candy bars are usually not lower in fat than chocolate bars. Although carob powder is low fat, the bars are not.

If you eat a high fat food item now and then, try to balance it with a low fat counterpart to average 15% to 18% fat per day.

18 x 2 = 36 Grams Of Fiber Per Day

Raw food is nature's broom to sweep the colon clean. If "an apple a day keeps the doctor away" it's most likely because of the fiber content in apples. Foods high in fiber take longer to chew, are low in fat and calories and fill the stomach with their volume. A full stomach signals to the brain a feeling of satiation. Fiber rich foods maintain blood sugar levels on an even keel, thus avoiding hunger pangs, irritability and a drop in energy. Besides helping to keep weight down, a high fiber diet can lower risk of heart disease and certain types of cancer.

There are two groups of fiber. Water-soluble fiber is predominant in apples, carrots, citrus fruits, bananas, oats, legumes and barley. This type of fiber helps lower cholesterol.

Water-insoluble fiber from wheat bran, whole wheat products, corn, lentils and brown rice provides bulk. This kind of fiber absorbs water in the digestive tract increasing in volume and cleansing the colon. It can help prevent constipation, colon cancer, diverticulosis and other intestinal disorders.

A person needs between 30 and 36 grams of fiber per day. As an average American, your fiber intake is probably between 12 and 16 grams a day. Increase fiber in your diet gradually to avoid cramps and bloating. Drink plenty of water.

To meet your fiber needs

- select whole grain products like whole wheat bread and brown rice
- eat beans, peas and lentils often
- choose fresh fruits and vegetables over canned
- leave the peel on fruits and vegetables if they are organically grown
- enjoy a salad every day
- snack on raw vegetables and fresh fruit
- use oats or bran as a filler in casseroles
- include a high fiber cereal daily
- eat an assortment of fibrous foods, not just bran

Some foods are more fibrous than others. A carrot contains twice as much fiber as a stalk of celery. An apple with skin has almost five times the fiber of a watermelon slice.

Fiber content of some foods in grams

6.8	Raspberries, raw	¾ cup
6.7	Blackberries, raw	¾ cup
5.8	Lentils, cooked	¾ cup
5.7	Peas, cooked	¾ cup
4.2	Corn, cooked	¾ cup
3.8	Strawberries	¾ cup
3.7	Apple, with skin	1 large
3.7	Carrot, raw	1 medium
3.7	Fig, dried	1 medium
3.6	Brown rice, cooked	¾ cup
3.2	Green beans, cooked	¾ cup
3.1	Spinach, cooked	¾ cup
3.1	Asparagus, cooked	¾ cup
3.0	Broccoli, cooked	¾ cup
3.0	Cranberries, raw	¾ cup
2.8	Pear, with skin	1 medium
2.8	Rolled oats, cooked	¾ cup
2.7	Kidney beans, cooked	¾ cup
2.4	Potato, cooked	¾ cup
2.1	Whole-meal bread	1 slice
2.1	Cabbage, raw	1 cup
1.9	Celery, raw	2 stalks

18 Hugs a week

There is only one happiness in life,
to love and to be loved.

George Sand

Hugging is 100% wholesome, naturally sweet and non-fattening. It helps our body's immune system, reduces stress and alleviates depression. Hugging helps the sick get healthy and the healthy get healthier. It is invigorating, rejuvenating and soothing. Anyone can hug. It feels good, is free and fully returnable.

Studies show that newborns do not develop well if they're not touched. Some babies die if not held, cuddled and loved. Preemies in incubators, who were massaged daily, developed better and could go home earlier than babies who were fed the same formula but not stroked. We never outgrow the need to be touched, the need for love and support. People who are ignored or seldom touched develop a sense of loneliness and begin to withdraw becoming even more lonely. Adults who do not get enough emotional strokes from touching might touch and eat food for comfort.

Giving and receiving hugs is a wonderful way to say, "You are OK, I love you." Regular hugs affirm and strengthen a relationship. Another form of hug is the emotional hug, to be there for someone, not only physically but emotionally and mentally as well. This enhances self-esteem, the way we feel about ourselves.

Lori, who came to Sans Souci for the second time to quit smoking, puzzled me. Usually our smoking cessation program is successful. After spending the time, energy and money to stop smoking at Sans Souci, why would she start again one year later?

An unusually beautiful and successful woman with a delightful sense of humor, Lori gave me the answer. "Susie," she said, "deep down, I feel that my cigarette and I deserve each other." After hearing that, I put away my latest manuals and tapes on smoking cessation and focused on her as the special, beautiful person she is, trying to convince her of her self-worth and uniqueness.

You, too, deserve to treat yourself right! There are many ways to do this. None of them include smoking or overeating on greasy cakes or candy bars. Neither does going on a guilt trip. Guilt is such a poor motivator. When it rears its ugly head, remind yourself that you have always, at every moment of your life, done the best that you could. You deserve neither reproach nor blame from anyone, including yourself. Thomas Edison tried over 5,000 times before he came up with the right filament for the light bulb. Instead of feeling guilty, you, too, can learn from your mistakes. A baby falls down many times before it learns to walk. You can risk taking a new step.

Develop your own credo, which you can repeat over and over in order to enhance your self esteem, and give yourself emotional hugs. Here is mine:

- I believe in myself. I believe that I am unique, physically, mentally and spiritually.
- I believe that life is a wonderful gift. It fills me with awe and wonder, and I give thanks to God and to my parents for the gift of life and love.
- I believe that the first responsibility towards this wonderful gift of life is to take care of it. Only to the degree that I am good to myself, can I be good to anyone else.
- I believe that my body is the temple for my soul. It is my duty to take care of it and to keep it free from abuse of any kind. I will eliminate destructive behaviors before they eliminate me.
- I believe that I have the power to focus on positive thoughts that affirm and nurture me. I can be true to myself.
- I believe that there is a special purpose for me on earth. In this great puzzle called life, there is a spot which only I can fill.
- I am committed to doing anything necessary to be well in body, mind and spirit.

What does it mean to be committed? In my native language there is no translation for this word, so I looked it up. Webster's dictionary says that a commitment is a pledge or promise. I like to add to this that commitment is a promise, backed up by action that takes us to the point of no return. A commitment sets in motion an energy of its own, but the crucial part is the action. This book will do nothing for you until you act on what you have learned from it. Act once or twice? No, act on it to the point of no return. Act over and over again, until it becomes second nature and you have developed a new habit.

When I ask guests at Sans Souci what time of the day their out-of-control snack-time is, the answer jumps out immediately, "in the evenings!" How many times do we go to the refrigerator with a full stomach, looking to fill an emptiness with the wrong food at the wrong time? At the end of a hectic day, with no time to meet our needs for touch and love, we create an emotional deficit. This imbalance can lead to depression, a life-threatening condition. Since food is always available and is one of our biggest pleasures and never rejects us, we reach out in the best way we know to get a fast "fix." It has worked in the past and for the moment it does the job. Comfort food once again restores our balance. As we scrape the last teaspoon out of the ice cream carton we feel better. A little overeating can't hurt, can it?

Oh yes, it can! The icy reality of our bathroom scale tells a different story. Being overweight adds insult to our bruised and neglected psyche. While contemplating the numbers on the scale, we look up and see our reflection in the mirror. Before remorse or guilt sends us all the way down into a dark depression, we catch ourselves by holding on to a piece of chocolate cake.

To break out of this self-defeating cycle takes support, motivation and knowledge. We can enlist the help of the three ego states described by Eric Berne in Transactional Analysis. The Parent gives nurturing support, the Child provides the motivation and the Adult shows step by step how it will be done. When all three parts of your personality agree, this autonomous decision is sure to make the winning difference.

Hunger is deeply personal and has many ways to manifest itself. If drawn toward a craving which calls for immediate gratification, ask what you are really hungry for, then seek the right nourishment. Love, friendship, a beautiful flower, a walk and talk with a friend or a hug might be what you really crave. Listen and trust yourself.

You can relearn to listen to the wisdom of your body. After years of neglecting the signals from overeating or from eating the wrong foods, your body shuts down. Someone who repeatedly touches hot surfaces becomes less sensitive to heat. Next time you feel out of sorts after that big, late dinner ask yourself the question, "What is my body telling me?"

Once you learn on an experiential level how good it feels to nurture yourself with the right food, exercise, emotional and physical hugs, you will want that feeling again and again. At Sans Souci, the love and support from our staff and from each guest is a crucial part in changing habits.

One of my guests sent me the following.

If I am not for myself - who will be for me?

If I am for myself alone - what am I?

If not now - when?

Hillel

CHAPTER 2
THE GOLDEN YEARS OF LIFE

*Those who love deeply never grow old;
they may advance in years,
but they stay young at heart.*

Sir Arthur Wing Pinero

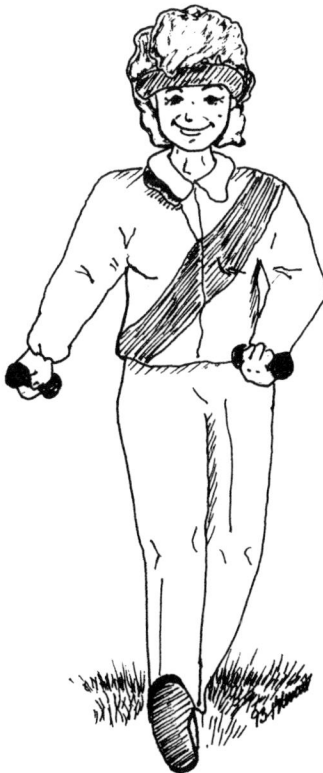

Today Americans live longer than ever before. Only two hundred years ago life spans averaged up to 35, today they have more than doubled. There are 3.3 million Americans over 85. Currently the number of Americans over the age of 65 is larger than the number of teenagers. Once you reach 65 the average life expectancy increases; for men 79 and for women 83.

With more years to live, our awareness focuses on increasing quality of life. Even with the best of care, bodies will undergo age-related changes. As we make adjustments to the physical changes, the power of our mind and spirit can rise. Free of the struggle for professional success, of the need to create and raise a family and to accumulate material goods, we can devote our time and energy to spiritual growth and to giving back to life and to society. With the kind of wisdom which can be gained only through living, maturity can be viewed as an ascending passage.

It is up to us to assure that age-related changes do not speed up to the point where we cannot enjoy the richness of a mature life. Indeed, I consider it a privilege to grow old. Though overall fitness may gradually decrease, I firmly believe that neither aging nor ultimately dying has to include getting sick. An active life style with physical and mental fitness and dietary adjustments can make mature age the most enjoyable part of our lives.

Our biological age can differ greatly from our chronological age. Markers of aging over which we have control are: skin health, cholesterol levels, blood pressure, muscle strength, muscle mass, aerobic capacity, body fat percentage and bone density. Changes in different body systems can be met in a constructive way.

The Skin

The most visible change during maturity is in the skin. Heredity and the way we take care of our skin determines its health and looks. We have no control over heredity, but there is much we can do about our life-style.

The major impact on skin aging is over-exposure to sun. We need light and sun for good health, but too much sun damages the skin. Tanned skin is damaged skin. The tan may disappear but the damage stays. The next tanning adds more damage. Resulting wrinkles are not the only drawback. Skin cancer through over-exposure to sun is the fastest growing cancer in our country. With more people going to the sunbelt and a decrease in the ozone layer it becomes vital to use sun screen, hats and clothing for protection.

Among the many damages caused by smoking is severe wrinkling of the skin. Smoking constricts peripheral blood vessels, deepening the wrinkles around eyes and mouth. This is also true of secondhand smoke.

A decrease in water content of body tissue produces difficulties in adjusting to sudden changes of temperature in the environment. This relative dehydration makes the skin look thinner and dryer as we age. Drinking enough liquids, avoiding harsh soaps and prolonged hot showers keeps the skin from drying out. Massaging the skin daily with Vaseline or a moisturizing lotion can be helpful.

The skin is our largest organ, with many critical functions. Massage increases blood flow, removes dead skin cells and reaches deep into our psyche. A massage given by a good massage therapist, is one of life's pleasures. Time and expense can limit this to an occasional treat, but there is no reason why we can't exchange neck and back massages with our partners or friends.

As an alternative, here is an-easy-to follow self-massage routine that can be done in five minutes with wonderful results. Start nude, massaging the back of your neck with one hand using firm horizontal strokes. Knead the right shoulder with your left hand. Gradually firm your grip repeating the kneading motion several times. Allow the muscles to fit into your palm, gently pulling upward. Oh...that feels good. Neck and shoulders tense up easily under stress. So linger on a bit and keep massaging this area enough to release tension. Repeat on the left shoulder. Good. Move on to your arms. Start with your right palm on the back of the left hand, stroking firmly upward on your arm toward the shoulder, bringing the blood towards the heart. Keeping in touch with your skin, gently stroke down toward the back of your hand. Repeat ten quick strokes. Do the same on the inside of your arm, pressing firmly going up and barely touching going down. Move to the other arm. Then massage the chest area with both palms in repeated horizontal strokes. As you massage the abdominal area, apply a firm pressure with both hands one on top of the other moving in clockwise circles. Reach your back by slapping the right shoulder area with the back of your left hand and massaging the strong muscle alongside your spine in a zig zag downward motion. Repeat several times on each side.

Massage your sides and waist line by placing both palms on your hips, moving them up and down your sides in opposite directions. Sway your body from side to side as you repeat ten times. Your legs are easy to massage. Using both hands, encircle your ankle with your palms and firmly stroke up towards your thighs and buttocks. Press firmly going up, barely touching moving down. Repeat ten strokes on each leg.

Take time for your feet. They serve you well all day and love to be touched. In a sitting position, massage each foot with both hands. Follow your intuition, massaging the ball of your foot, the arch and the heel. Apply pressure on the ball of the foot with your thumb, then massage each toe separately. Do this massage routine in the morning before your shower. It limbers and warms you up. Circle your foot in its full range of motion. Point and flex your foot ten times.

If you want to go one step further toward a wonderful alive feeling, follow your regular warm shower with a short cool or cold shower. Never take a cold shower if you are shivering or feeling cold. It takes some time to get used to the cold water. After a warm shower, start by exposing your arms for 5 seconds to the cold water. After doing this for a few weeks, do the same with your legs and eventually the whole body. After a while you will not want to miss the wonderful alive feeling a cold shower gives you. It improves your blood circulation and increases your resistance to colds. Father Kneip, a German priest, transformed his hometown Worishofen, Germany, into a well-known health resort for hydro-therapy. He founded his successful treatments on applications of cold water, saying: "What cold water cannot cure, only the knife can cure."

Nutrition

Eating right is a lifelong commitment that pays particular dividends in the later years of life. Good eating habits can help the older person maintain a high level of function and reduce the risk related to cardio-vascular disease, cancer, obesity and diabetes. After the age of 30 years, the metabolic rate declines 3% per decade leading to a reduced caloric need. A tendency to gain weight can be counteracted with dietary adjustments and a regular exercise program.

As we grow older our organs change, making it critical to focus on good nutrition to support health and quality of life. For example, an 80-year-old person experiences a 65% decrease in the number of taste buds, making it harder to taste food. To compensate for this, many older people add more sugar and salt to get the same amount of pleasure from eating. However, with progressing years, our bodies don't handle simple sugars well. If a young person and an older person each eats the same amount of cake, the blood sugar level of the older person tends to stay higher for a longer time. A prolonged elevated blood sugar level can promote diabetes which in turn can damage blood vessels and eyesight.

Simple sugars, called simple carbohydrates, like table sugar and honey add calories, but few if any other nutrients. Calorie requirements may shrink as we age, but not the need for vitamins, minerals and protein. Therefore, we have to get more nutrients out of less food. We can accomplish this by avoiding simple carbohydrates and fats and choosing more complex carbohydrates like whole grains, vegetables and fruits.

The tendency to add more salt to food can contribute to high blood pressure and electrolyte imbalance. Try herbs and spices instead of salt. They add pleasure and variety to your meals with no nasty side effects. Aging doesn't change our protein requirements but some physical problems do. Acute or chronic illnesses and surgery can increase the need for protein. Good sources of protein, besides fish, chicken and turkey breast, are low fat milk products and legumes.

As we mature, it becomes crucial to eat ample fiber. Proper bowel function and a healthy colon depend on sufficient fiber. Fiber also helps lower blood cholesterol levels and keeps blood sugar levels at a more even keel.

Together with a high fiber food intake it is crucial to drink enough water. With advanced age there is a tendency to neglect liquids which leads to dehydration. Some cases of confusion in the elderly can be reversed by simply rehydrating the body.

The most important age-related dietary change is to reduce total fat intake, especially saturated fats. A high fat diet stimulates the liver to produce more cholesterol which, in turn, may clog arteries. If the long term benefits of a low fat diet seem remote, keep in mind that consuming a high-fat meal leads to high blood levels of fat only hours following the meal. This higher level of fat in the blood could trigger a blood vessel to clog up. The risk of a heart attack after a fatty meal, especially in the more mature population, is higher because blood vessels might already be narrowed. In addition a high fat meal makes most of us feel heavy and sluggish for hours after it has been consumed. Benefits of a low fat diet are immediate and long term. Choosing a salad, broccoli and plain baked potato with fish may bring you benefits today and ten years ahead.

Some older women and men tend to have diets low in zinc and vitamin D. Foods rich in zinc are legumes, seafood, meat, milk and eggs. Vitamin D is found in fortified milk, tuna and salmon. The body is able to make Vitamin D with exposure to sun light.

In summary, eating a variety of foods high in complex carbohydrates and fiber, moderate in protein and low in fat and salt can help us stay healthy well into a mature age. With advancing years, it makes more sense to reduce or eliminate caffeine, alcohol, sugar, white flour, visible fats and salt. Recipes in this book are nutrient dense and combine flavor-enhancing herbs and spices to transform each meal into an enjoyable experience.

Bones and Muscles

Although osteoporosis is more common in women over 50, men are also affected. Weight bearing exercises like walking or resistance training can increase bone density and/or lessen bone loss, counteracting osteoporosis. By strengthening muscles the likelihood of falls and bone fractures decreases greatly.

For strong bones exercise regularly and give your body adequate amounts of calcium, vitamin D, magnesium and zinc. In addition to milk and milk products, good sources of calcium are green leafy vegetables, legumes, almonds, bony fish and calcium fortified products like some fruit juices and cereals.

Women over 50 can contribute to bone health by taking 1000 to 1500 milligrams of calcium supplements per day. Vitamin C rich foods help absorption of calcium. Taking part of the calcium in the evening may help you sleep better. Don't take more than 500 milligrams at one time. If you take your calcium pill with lemon water, the acidity will help break it down in the stomach, enhancing absorption. Smoking, alcohol, caffeine containing drinks, laxative abuse, restrictive fad diets and high protein diets deplete the body of calcium.

The decrease in muscle tissue observed in older people seems to be related to inactivity more than to age. Recent studies show that 80- and 90-year-old folks are able to increase their muscle strength by exercising regularly. A regular fitness program is vitally important as we mature. Exercise reduces the risk of cardiovascular disease, increases stamina and well being. It improves sleep, counteracts depression and makes us look and feel better. As we mature we need to give exercise a high priority. How high? As high as you can - like eating and sleeping for example.

Joint mobility tends to diminish with age but can be greatly improved with a regular stretching and toning program. Inactivity is the surest way toward joint and cartilage degeneration. Exercise enhances the blood supply to joints, bringing oxygen and nourishment to them. By strengthening joints and muscles we can keep them healthy and functional well into old age.

Aerobic exercise helps to facilitate the delivery and utilization of oxygen in the brain. This enhances brain function and reaction time. During exercise the brain also releases endorphins, a powerful mood elevator.

A simple program of walking, stretching and toning brings benefits to all ages, but is a must at maturity. Be gentle with yourself and listen to your body. Doing too much too soon does more harm than good. It takes time to build stamina. Detailed information on how to start an exercise program is in Chapter One.

I cannot close this chapter without a word on spine health. We are supported in an upright position by our muscles. Therefore, it is important to strengthen back muscles through walking and toning exercises. For a healthy back, it is just as important to keep abdominal muscles toned and to maintain a good posture. The tendency to slouch forward can have devastating consequences as we age. To assure good posture, hold your shoulders back and downward with your head up and your stomach pulled in. Visualize a rope pulling you upward and lengthening your spine. It looks and feels good to stand tall, taking up your rightful space in the universe. Regret not growing older - it is a privilege denied to many.

Joy and Love

Laughter and joy enhance the immune system and promote the production of endorphins. Endorphins are powerful chemicals that make you feel good. Laughter is a tranquilizer with no side effects. Laughter and love are true youth elixirs.

There is wisdom in looking at a plant with many thorns and one flower and calling it a rosebush. Look for beauty in life and spread love around you rather than focus on pain. The highest form of love is to support the person you love, and a good place to start is with yourself. You can love others only to the degree that you love yourself. Experiencing love and acceptance produces a special peace and joy which measurably changes the body's chemistry towards health and wholeness. The ultimate lesson in life is love.

CHAPTER 3
HABIT CONTROL FOR HEALTH AND HAPPINESS
by
Jeneene Brengelman, Ph.D.

We eat what we eat because we got in the habit of eating that way. As children, we formed habits based on what our parents ate or what "special" foods we got or wanted. Most of us were rewarded with sweet, fatty foods, and many of us were coerced to eat salty, overcooked vegetables. Things either tasted good or were good for us, rarely both. When we sit down at the table as adults, we bring the child we were along with us. Food is an important part of family history. If we liked Uncle Joe and he peppered his tomatoes, we might do that. If we didn't like him, we might not eat tomatoes at all. Eggs are a treat to me no matter the hour. When my Uncle Ed came home from his travels, he'd take us kids out to breakfast, and we'd order eggs. How many ways can you think of, both healthy and unhealthy, that your childhood continues to affect your eating habits?

Most of us have a habit or two that we'd like to change. Research shows that it takes from 21 to 28 days to change a habit. I always give it a month. You are changing your mind, your subconscious mind, and there are no shortcuts. There is a key, and I call it the CAR key.

Commitment + Action = Results

We all want to eat better and exercise more, but there's always an excuse to delay change. Commitment means that you give your word to do something even when you're tired, even when you forget why you wanted to do it in the first place. You do it because you promised, period. Action means that you start that commitment now, that you be in action no matter what your thoughts are doing. If you repeat the action every day for a month, you will have created a new habit.

Remember when you learned to type? You had to repeat the motions over and over consciously, until they became subconscious. You repeated the action and you were committed to learning it. The same was true of learning to drive, or skate, or ride a bike. Commitment plus repeated action gave you the results you wanted.

Once you make the commitment to change a habit you can make it easier by giving yourself the gift of positive self-talk. You may be in the habit of eating sweet desserts and want to start eating fruit. If you tell yourself it's a sacrifice, your mind will resist this change. You may eat the fruit, but you'll still want a sweet dessert, and feel deprived when you don't get it. Instead, buy yourself beautiful fruit. Choose each piece with care and serve it on a china plate with a special knife. Eat it slowly and let your self-talk be peaceful and positive. Do this for a month, and you will have changed your mind and your habit.

Health makes it easier to be happy, and happiness makes it easier to be healthy. In fact, without good health it's very hard to be happy. Without happiness our health suffers. Still, many of us cling to unhealthy habits because at one time in our lives they were associated with happiness. I think it's safe to say that for most of us, eating and exercise habits are based more on the pursuit of happiness than on the pursuit of health. A good affirmation for changing your mind about how to be happy is:

> *True happiness comes with treating my body as a valued friend. Peace enhances the flavor of healthy foods. Unhealthy foods bring anxiety. I choose peace.*

Put that affirmation on a card on your table, and read it every day for a month. The first few times it might sound silly or untrue for you. After a week or so you'll begin to notice the feelings of peace or anxiety that come with your food choices. That recognition will make it easier for you to see that happiness lies in learning healthier eating habits.

Changing your eating habits at mealtimes and controlling between-meal snacks are distinct from each other and require different strategies for habit control. Changing mealtime eating habits is fairly straightforward. Make a commitment to eat three servings of vegetables and fruits as part of each dinner and no visible fat for a month. After the month is over those will be habits. You won't have to think about those any more and you can start something new. Next you might decide to add more fiber to your diet, gradually so your stomach adjusts to it. You buy the proper foods and consciously remind yourself every day for a month, keep up the positive self-talk and that becomes a habit.

Now let's talk about between-meal eating. This is more of a challenge because we eat between meals for many reasons. Hunger can be triggered by seeing an advertisement for food on TV or hearing the bell of the ice cream truck. Many of us eat between meals because we feel sad. "This cookie will make you feel better" was part of most people's childhood. As adults, we eat a whole package of cookies and are convinced it makes us feel better. In fact it was your mother's caring and attention that made you feel better, but the cookie was, and still is, the symbol.

Comfort foods such as cookies and ice cream become habits because we see them as quick sources of comfort. Unfortunately, they don't really satisfy, so we eat more and more. If vegetable soup is your comfort food, no problem. But if your comfort food is overloaded with sugar and fat, it might be a habit worth breaking. Look for patterns. If you find yourself eating ice cream in the evening when you're alone, try calling someone at that time instead. Human beings were not designed to be alone. We couldn't even think alone because we wouldn't have a vocabulary with which to think without others. We are social and yet we Americans idealize independence. This isolation makes for some unhappy, unhealthy humans. Just talking with another person will make you feel better because talking releases endorphins, the feel-good, keep feeling good, chemical in your brain.

Laughter does it too, so share a joke or even a comic strip on your call. You do get endorphins from eating those favorite foods. There are several other ways to get them. You can replace your between meal bad eating habits with any of the ingredients in what I call "Jeneene's Ten Million Dollar Recipe for Happiness" which I'll give you for free! The magic word is SLERTT, and it stands for Sex, Laughter, Exercise, Relaxation, Talking and Touching.

Exercise is the most dramatic endorphin producer, but the others are great too. Taking a walk, calling someone, relaxing in a warm bath, all produce a very real sense of well-being. They might take a little more thought than eating a candy bar but the rewards are both immediate and permanent. You empower yourself every time you make a healthy choice and that empowerment makes the next healthy choice easier.

Don't eat after 7 P.M. Susie says food eaten then counts double. It makes sense, because you are resting before your body has a chance to metabolize food eaten late in the evening. When I feel the nighttime hungries I've made it a habit to look back at the food I've eaten all day to assure myself that I don't need food. I acknowledge myself for feeling hungry and not rushing to the fridge. Now that's usually enough, but while the habit was forming I had to be more creative with self-talk and distractions, such as frozen grapes.

Water is therapeutic in many ways. Drinking more of it is a great habit to develop. The old trick of filling a pitcher and pouring glassfuls from it to see your intake and push you to drink more is a good one. Keeping a 1-liter bottle with you wherever you go, especially in the car, will have the same effect. Refill it twice a day. If you don't like the taste of city water, buy a purifier or bottled water, add lemon or a splash of juice.

Buy yourself flowers. Use your nicest dishes, even when you're alone. Treating your body gently, giving it the foods it needs for optimal health, is being good to yourself. You are using the wisdom you have as an adult to change habits that you formed as a child. Then fatty foods were part of special times. Now you can create those special memories around the foods that truly nurture you. If you've been to Sans Souci, you have some of those memories. You can give yourself more by turning off the TV, lighting a candle, and having a flower on the table when you sit down to eat. Remember, you are changing your mind and that takes commitment and repeated action.

Alcohol is another thing that most of us have deceived ourselves about for years. Fact is, alcohol is very unflattering and it breaks the brakes. After a drink or two, we forget all our good intentions. Alcohol damages your liver and brain. Especially if you feel you need a drink to enjoy yourself, leaving alcohol in the past is a good idea. Order a delicious juice drink and get high on self-esteem. Try cranberry juice with club soda.

Stress is another problem that causes some of us to make unhealthy choices. Life is unpredictable, and often it defies our plans. Feeling out of control creates stress. Learning new habits to control stress can help you lengthen your life as well as control your weight. Stress is a physical response to a perceived danger. Our bodies were designed to release adrenaline in response to danger. Adrenaline gives us the quick strength to fight or flee. It is a powerful mix of chemicals, most of which are not damaging in small quantities. Problem is, we no longer confront a tiger once a month. Now we feel stress most of every day and in large quantities those chemicals become dangerous. If you can lighten up, if you can leave some of your perfectionism behind, you'll feel better and live longer. A good affirmation for less stress is:

> *I am a perfectly designed imperfect human being. There are no mistakes in life, only challenges and lessons to be learned. I trust the perfect unfolding of my life.*

After a month just say,

> *This place on the path is perfect.*

Now I'll share with you the most fun habit to make. Live passionately! Living passionately means buying, eating, doing only those things you passionately want to buy, eat or do. It means living each day fully, paying attention to your body and your spirit, and going to bed at night feeling good about yourself. When you passionately want something, you eat every bite with joy, giving it the attention it deserves. Then, when you no longer passionately want the next bite, you stop! No more eating because it's in front of you or somebody fixed it just for you. You are now willing to protect your body passionately!

Make this habit yours by asking yourself these questions: Do I passionately want this? Do I want it passionately enough to be willing to wear it forever if it's fatty? If the answer is no, act quickly. Don't let your mind make excuses for this one time. You can have reasons or you can have results but not both.

You can never get enough of what you don't really want. If you want comfort and you eat, you'll stay hungry. Since food isn't what you really want, it can never satisfy you. If you feel lonely, sad, or angry, call someone. Food will only make you feel worse. In motivating yourself to change habits it's good to remember that *this moment counts.*

We all have great plans for someday, but someday isn't on any calendar. There won't come a time when all the stresses are gone. There will never be a day when the french fries you do or don't eat will show immediately on your body. It's so easy to put off making changes because we want to feel good now.

Here's how to feel good now. Acknowledge yourself fully for every healthy choice. Self-esteem feels better than the aftertaste of sugar. Acknowledge yourself immediately and lovingly. Don't be modest. You are changing your mind and the words you use matter. You can begin today to give yourself large portions of self-confidence. When you don't make the healthy choice, forgive yourself and reaffirm your commitment to your health and happiness. Look at what went wrong and come up with a plan to get back on track.

Don't let yourself get too hungry, angry, lonely or tired. Treat yourself gently.

Health and inner peace are gifts only you can give yourself and they are the finest treasures of all. Making healthy choices and turning those choices into habits will enrich every day of your life. It's never too late to begin again. As Shakespeare said, "What's past is prologue." The future is yours!

Jeneene Brengelman, Ph.D. teaches smoking cessation and habit control at Sans Souci. She is in private practice as a personal health consultant in Cincinnati, Ohio. Her goal is to help people learn to love themselves enough to stop hurting themselves.

CHAPTER 4
VITAL VITAMINS
by
Carol Soehner, RD

From pure joy springs all creation,
by joy it is sustained,
toward joy it proceeds and to joy it returns.

When you think about vitamins what comes to your mind? When I ask this question of my friends, the reply is often, "Pills" or "Children need them to grow." Some even answered, "Well, which vitamin are you talking about? Don't they all have different purposes within the body?" These were all good responses and I know if I continued to survey others, I would get an even greater variety of answers.

These people were all accurate in their visions of vitamins. Health and happiness are the prizes we earn when we learn how to eat wisely. We eat for enjoyment, to fuel our bodies and to provide the nutrients we need for good health. We call those nutrients vitamins and minerals.

Vitamins and minerals are essential to health and well-being. They aid the body in the breakdown of foods and help change the food into a form that it can use to perform its everyday activities. Minerals allow the body to maintain a balance of fluids and help develop and maintain bones, muscles and nerves. The human body needs a variety of foods to function. The quest is to "seek and find" the different types of vitamins and minerals that will make our bodies "go."

The grocery store is like a maze with an enormous selection of foods. How to find the right foods is the puzzle, just like a "seek and find." The wide variety of foods to choose from can cause confusion. The object of our "seek and find" is to eliminate those foods that are low in nutritional value or "distractors."

There are two different types of vitamins, fat-soluble and water-soluble vitamins. The four fat-soluble vitamins, A, D, E and K that can be stored within the body's fat cells. Since they do not dissolve in water they can't be eliminated through the kidneys, as can water-soluble vitamins. Therefore, an excess of fat-soluble vitamins can build up to harmful levels in the body. Check with your nurse or dietitian before taking these vitamins.

The water-soluble vitamins include B vitamins and vitamin C. These vitamins are not stored in the body and must be replenished on a daily basis. Now that we know what we are looking for, we have to be able to identify the nourishing foods from the "distractor" foods. As a general rule of thumb look for fresh colorful vegetables and fruits. The fresher the better. Long storage, cutting, heating or otherwise processing will destroy some or all of the vitamins. Sugar, white flour, polished rice, oils, margarines and most other fats have few or no vitamins and minerals. We call them empty calories.

FAT-SOLUBLE VITAMINS

VITAMIN A is essential in development and function of our eyes. Without vitamin A, we would not be able to adjust to light changes, either extreme brightness or darkness. It is also important in maintaining healthy skin, hair, teeth and bones. Vitamin A allows our bodies to fight off infections and sicknesses. Research studies are beginning to show that it may play a part in cancer prevention.

Look for color in vegetables and fruits. The darker green or yellow the color the more vitamin A it contains. For example, pink grapefruit contains more vitamin A than white grapefruit; dark blue grapes have more vitamin A than white; cantaloupe more than honeydew and romaine lettuce contains more vitamin A than iceberg lettuce. Other examples of foods that are rich in vitamin A include yellow and dark green leafy vegetables and fruits, such as carrots, collards, spinach, sweet potatoes, squash, broccoli, apricots, peaches and oranges.

VITAMIN D is associated with skeletal growth, strong bones and teeth. Vitamin D also helps with the absorption and retention of calcium within the body. Today, there are few cases of vitamin D deficiency. This may be attributed to developments of modern technology about vitamin D fortification of different foods. In addition, your body can make vitamin D with exposure to sun. The Food and Nutrition Board, National Academy of Sciences-National Research Council, does not have a recommended daily allowance, RDA, vitamin D. You can get enough vitamin D through exposure to sun light and by eating fish/seafood, vitamin D fortified milk, and certain cereal grains. You may need supplemental vitamin D if you are house bound for lengthy periods of time.

VITAMIN E acts as a protector of vitamin A and the essential fatty acids. Vitamin E also plays a role in the creation of red-blood cells, muscles, and other tissues within the body. In addition, vitamin E helps regulate blood-pressure. In the past decade, many different health claims have sprouted about vitamin E. These include increased fertility or prevention of sterility, relief of menstrual disorders, and prevention of ischemic heart disease. None of these claims can actually be proven. Vitamin E occurs abundantly in every division of the food pyramid. Some examples of foods rich in Vitamin E include soy and kidney beans, different types of nuts, carrots, corn, spinach, eggs, beef, herring, also cereal grains, such as barley, rye and whole grain wheat.

VITAMIN K is formed within the intestine. Its primary function is to prevent losing blood through the cuts and scrapes that we incidentally gain throughout our lives. Thus, vitamin K is responsible for clotting our blood. Dietary sources of vitamin K are broccoli, cabbage, spinach, lettuce, brussel sprouts, turnip greens, asparagus, bananas, strawberries, oats and whole wheat. Vitamin K deficiency is unlikely to occur. However, antibiotics tend to destroy the conditions in the large intestine that vitamin K formation needs. Therefore, when a person is on antibiotics, it is important to consume an ample supply of green leafy vegetables and low-fat yogurt.

WATER-SOLUBLE VITAMINS

VITAMIN B has various forms that are often spoken of as a group, otherwise known as the B complex vitamins. These vitamins work together to help break down carbohydrates, protein, and fat into usable forms.

Good sources of the different forms of vitamin B are whole grains, enriched breads and cereals, non-fat or low-fat cheese, low-fat cottage cheese, lean meats, fish and dried beans and peas. If you are consuming a wide variety of foods from each of the food pyramid groups, there is a good chance that you get all the B vitamins you need. However, if you are a strict vegetarian and eat only plant products, you might have problems consuming enough foods that contain an adequate amount of vitamin B 12 and B 6. Supplementation may become necessary because these B vitamins occur in abundance in foods that are from animal sources.

VITAMIN C helps the body absorb iron, and to heal cuts and wounds. Before the discovery of America when people were traveling across the ocean, sailors and travelers prevented scurvy by consuming lemons. They learned this through experience but it was not until 1932 that vitamin C deficiency was discovered as the cause of scurvy. Some studies show that vitamin C has the ability to reduce the severity and length of time common colds. Good sources of vitamin C are citrus fruits, raw green leafy vegetables, strawberries, papaya, tomatoes and green bell peppers.

During different periods of our lives, our bodies require different amounts of nutrients. For example, active young children need more of the various vitamins and minerals than adults. At times of stress or illness the body requires larger amounts of B vitamins. Older people may need more calcium. To eat for health and happiness, we should choose nutrient dense foods, low in fat and calories, foods that are abundant in vitamins and minerals. Such foods would include a variety of fruits, vegetables and grains. They are great tasting and easy to prepare.

CHAPTER 5
SANS SOUCI FOOD PLAN

*Now and then it is good to pause
in the pursuit of happiness and just be happy.*

Chinese proverb

Our body needs carbohydrates, protein, fat, vitamins, minerals, water and fiber. We can get these from a variety of vegetables, legumes, grains, fruits and nuts. Combinations of grains and legumes provide a complete protein with all the essential amino acids. They are higher in nutrients and lower in fat than meat and cheese and, of course, like all plant food have no cholesterol.

More than half of the world's population eats meat sparingly or not at all. They tend to have a lower incidence of cardiovascular disease and cancer than we have. Small amounts of animal protein can be used to flavor vegetables and grains instead of making it the center of a meal.

As a basic principle choose food low in fat, high in complex carbohydrates and moderate in protein.

Practice variety and moderation in food consumption. Overeating, even on healthy foods, is taxing your body. Consume most of your calories before 7 P.M. Drink 6 to 8 glasses of water a day. If you choose fruit juices, dilute them with water. Whole fruits are preferable because of their fiber content, pleasure in chewing and filling power.

Desirable foods

whole grain products made with wheat, spelt, brown rice, corn, rolled oats, millet, buckwheat, amaranth, legumes like beans, lentils, peas vegetables like carrots, cauliflower, broccoli, cabbage, brussels sprouts, peppers, asparagus, squash, potatoes greens like parsley, water cress, kale, collard - turnip -mustard greens, spinach, leafy green lettuce fruits like melons, berries, peaches, citrus, apples, pears

If you are on a weight reduction program,
limit to two fruits a day.

Foods to consume in moderate amounts

fish, turkey, skinless chicken, low fat milk products,
seeds, nuts

Foods to avoid or use seldom

fried food, fat in all its visible forms, cured meats,
bacon, sugar, white flour, caffeine containing drinks,
salt, alcohol, overly processed foods,
whole milk products, red meat

FOOD PYRAMID

The new food pyramid, published by the Department of Agriculture, stresses grains, vegetables and fruit as the basis of a healthy diet.

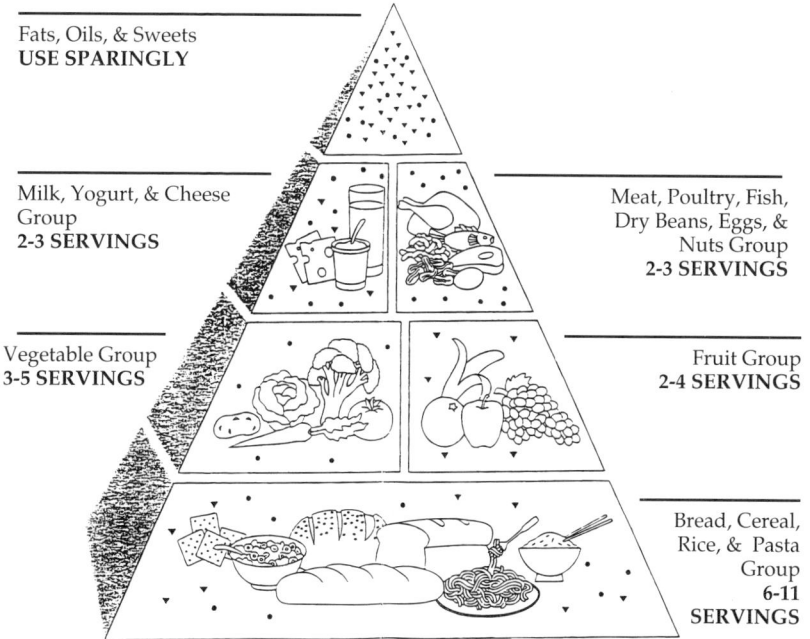

Fats, Oils, & Sweets
USE SPARINGLY

Milk, Yogurt, & Cheese Group
2-3 SERVINGS

Meat, Poultry, Fish, Dry Beans, Eggs, & Nuts Group
2-3 SERVINGS

Vegetable Group
3-5 SERVINGS

Fruit Group
2-4 SERVINGS

Bread, Cereal, Rice, & Pasta Group
6-11 SERVINGS

Key
- Fat (naturally occurring and added)
▼ Sugars (added)

SANS SOUCI FOOD CHART

COMPLEX CARBOHYDRATES:
70%

PROTEIN:
12%

FAT:
18%

CARBOHYDRATES
Whole Grains:
- oats
- wheat
- brown rice
- buckwheat
- rye
- corn

Legumes:
- beans
- peas
- lentils
- peanuts

Vegetables:
- potatoes
- cabbage
- broccoli
- cauliflower
- carrots

Fruits:
- melons
- berries
- peaches
- apples
- citrus

PROTEINS
- combinations of legumes and grains
- fish, poultry, eggs
- low fat dairy

FATS:
- all of the above
- nuts
- seeds
- avocados

This food chart suggests that 70% of total calories come from carbohydrates, 12% from protein and 18% of total calories from fat. In our daily lives, the best we can do is to approximate these percentages. Most food items combine carbohydrates, fats and protein. For example, beans contain carbohydrates, proteins and fat. The same goes for grains. As the protein is not complete, combining a grain and a legume makes for a complete protein. Similarly, everything we eat from nature's kitchen provides some fat, even fruits and vegetables. This chart shows you where you want to place the main focus in your food selections.

CHAPTER 6

SUGGESTIONS FOR FOOD PREPARATION

Organizing your Kitchen

*People more attention pay,
to what you do than what you say.*

Some of my suggestions may require adjustments in your kitchen. Clean out your cupboards of all fattening foods which you no longer want to become part of your body. Consider giving away those foods that you will no longer use, so you won't be tempted to justify using them all up before starting the plan. In addition to the obvious, equip your kitchen with.

- cheese funnel • steamer • blender • sprouting jars and tops
  - food processor • hot-air popper • nonstick pans
  - lettuce spinner • measuring cups • kitchen scale

Place special emphasis on low fat, eliminating or reducing all forms of processed, visible fats. Although vegetable oils are better than lard or butter, they are processed, concentrated foods like sugar or white flour and have little nutrient value. The oil in a sunflower seed is protected from getting rancid by the seed's skin. When the protective covering is removed from the seed, the contact with air begins oxidizing the oil, making it rancid. It may take weeks or months for the oil to taste or smell rancid, but the process starts right after the initial pressing. Adding seed to your meals instead of oils brings many benefits. They taste better, provide vitamins, minerals, protein, fiber and all the fat you need. Instead of sunflower oil in salad dressings, try adding sunflower seed or sprouted sunflower seed on salads. Instead of olive oil, add olives, try avocado instead of bacon bits.

How do you cook without butter and oil? Read on - that's what the recipes in this book are all about. There is pleasure and nurturing nutrition in eating life-giving whole foods. Start by making a weekly menu and market order. Do not shop when hungry or tired. Take advantage of locally grown fresh fruits and vegetables. To avoid impulse buying and save time, you might try to order groceries by phone for home delivery. Keep a calorie counter, kitchen scale, and measuring cups on hand until you learn to estimate quantities and calories. You don't have to count every calorie, but calories do count. Learn which are the low calorie choices.

Start every meal with a raw, "sun cooked" item, like a salad, fresh vegetables or fruit. This fills you up on high volume, nutrient dense and low fat food. It aids digestion and keeps your waistline slender. Eating food close to its natural state keeps the nutrients intact and assures maximum health and energy. Heat destroys some vitamins. The longer you cook or otherwise process food, the fewer vitamins remain. At Sans Souci we have developed 5 methods to shorten cooking time and preserve nutrients:

1. Soak grains and legumes for 8 hours or overnight before cooking. By soaking brown rice for example, I cut down cooking time from 45 minutes to 10 minutes. I cook rice in its soak-

ing water.   By contrast, if I soak beans, I replace the soaking water with fresh water before cooking to avoid flatulence.

2. Cut down on cooking time by simply doing just that, cook less.   For example, we cook our Sans Souci vegetable soup only 5 to 8 minutes, leaving the vegetables still crunchy.

3. Simplify cooking.   Broil, steam, poach, grill or bake instead of frying.   Modify your favorite recipes.   For example: use vegetable broth or butter-flavor granules to replace oil or butter; powdered skim milk or evaporated skim milk instead of cream; vegetable stock instead of beef stock; frozen apple juice concentrate, undiluted instead of sugar; cooked and pureed vegetables instead of gravy.   Cut out salt and use herbs, spices or extracts for taste.

4. Cook once, serve twice.   It takes almost the same amount of time to cook double batches.   Foods that freeze well are casseroles, soups, bran muffins and most cooked meats.   Some foods do not freeze well.   Eggs are better fresh.   Most potatoes and pastas taste better when fresh cooked.   It doesn't take long to learn what freezes well.   Label packages with the type of food, the number of servings and the date you prepared it.   Store food in air tight containers.   Storage time for soups and casseroles is up to three months, for bread and muffins up to two months, and for sandwiches one month.

5. Last but not least, don't cook.   Eat one meal a day raw, "sun cooked" or "sun ripened."   One of my favorite lunches is half a cantaloupe with 2 tablespoons of Fitness Cheese and Essene bread, or a large mixed salad with a baked potato topped with Fitness Cheese and chives.   Soak and wash vegetables and fruits thoroughly before using them.

Whenever possible use fresh herbs instead of the dried variety, fresh garlic instead of garlic powder and fresh onions instead of onion powder.   I also prefer freshly squeezed lemon juice instead of the bottled juice.   Keep vegetable soup or the calcium booster soup, bran muffins, fruits, fresh vegetables with Sans Souci dip or seed sauce on hand for times when you are hit by a "snack attack."

Use hard cheeses for seasoning only, rather than as a food, because of their high salt and fat content.   Soak feta cheese in water for one to two hours to reduce salt.   Cooking the Sans Souci way becomes easier with practice. It takes three to four weeks to form a new habit. "Practice Makes Permanent."

When serving food remember that we also eat with our eyes. Decorate the plates with parsley, mint leaves, cherry tomatoes, julienned vegetables, colorful fruit or edible blossoms like violets, marigolds and rose petals.

Eat breakfast like a Queen/King
share lunch with a friend
give dinner to your enemies

European proverb

Herb Magic

Each time you say
can't" , you are trapped.
instead, "I can and I will"

The use of herbs and spices is a matter of individual taste. When I asked the chef of our local four-star restaurant, L'Auberge, if he measures and weighs for his gourmet cooking he replied, "Susie, good cooking comes from the gut, not from the head. I never measure seasonings." You can create your own favorite way to season food.

If you can't find certain products like Jensen's Broth, use Hauser's Broth or any other low-sodium vegetable broth. Alternately, you can ask your local grocery or health food store to order the products you need. I choose many seasonings and spices for their taste appeal and nutritional value. Here are some of my favorite ways to season.

CHIVES: Fresh chopped or dried. Add to soups, egg white omelettes, Sans Souci Fitness Cheese, baked pota-to or casseroles

GARLIC: Use fresh, as garlic powder or garlic paste. I use it in soups, vegetable dishes, Italian, Mexican or Oriental recipes

DILL: Stem, leaves, flowers, seed. Enlivens almost any vegetable. Add to vinegar, soup, or fish. Boil a small amount with cabbage, turnips or cauliflower

CARAWAY: Seed. Mix with Sans Souci Fitness Cheese as a bread spread or cooked vegetables for crunch

PARSLEY: Leaves. Add to soups, casseroles, boiled vegetables, sprinkle on salad or use as garnish

MARJORAM: Leaves, flower heads. Add to soups, tomatoes, peas, potatoes, casseroles, salads

BASIL: Leaves. Good on tomato, squash, salads, omelettes, and soups

THYME: Leaves. Add a pinch to enliven any soup, casserole or fish

TARRAGON: Leaves. Add directly to vinegar or to salads. Use in legumes, fish or baked chicken

PEPPERMINT, SPEARMINT: Leaves. Brew as tea, add to vinegar, excellent with fruit, use fresh leaves for flavoring ice drinks, use for Tabbouli

Spices And Seasonings

JENSEN'S BROTH: Its salt-like taste comes from dehydrated celery. Enhances almost any vegetable, fish or chicken dish

VEGIT: A vegetable seasoning I use for most casseroles and soups. In recipes vegetable seasoning mix is the term used for this product

MRS. DASH: An excellent salt substitute with a zing to it. In recipes herb seasoning mix is the term used for this product

QUICK-SIP: A liquid vegetable seasoning. Excellent for chicken, vegetables, and soups. Use instead of soy sauce

BRAGG LIQUID AMINOS: Similar to Quick-Sip

LOW-SODIUM SOY SAUCE: Liquid salt substitute

BUTTER BUDS: A natural butter-like flavor, use sparingly in the beginning and eventually replace it with herbs and spices. In recipes butter-flavor granules is the term used for this product

CINNAMON: Wonderful with apple, squash, cantaloupe

CURRY POWDER: Good with chicken and rice

BLACKSTRAP MOLASSES: Nutritious sweetener

BARLEY MALT and HONEY: Sweetens more than sugar, use sparingly

LEMON JUICE: Enhances flavor of almost anything

PAM: One of the no stick cooking sprays. I prefer Pam Olive Oil Cooking Spray. In recipes cooking spray is the term used for this product

NUTMEG: Good with fruit, squash, muffins

PAPRIKA: Chicken, Fitness Cheese, potato

GARLIC BREAD SPRINKLE: Enhances potato chips or bread

Good Combinations

TOMATOES: Dill, basil, marjoram, onion, oregano

ASPARAGUS: Lemon juice, onion, garlic, vinegar

CHICKEN: Curry, green bell pepper, lemon juice, marjoram, fresh mushrooms, paprika, parsley, poultry seasoning, sage, thyme, dill

CUCUMBERS: Dill, garlic, vinegar, fresh lime juice, onion

FISH: Tarragon, bay leaf, curry powder, dry mustard powder, green bell pepper, lemon juice, marjoram, fresh mushrooms, paprika, carrot, onion

GREEN BEANS: Dill, lemon juice, marjoram, nutmeg, pimento, onion

GREENS: Onion, garlic, pepper, vinegar, Bragg Liquid Aminos

CORN: Green bell pepper, pimento, fresh tomato, sage, dill

RICE: Ginger, chives, green bell pepper, onion, pimento, curry, cumin, saffron

PEAS: Mint, fresh mushrooms, onion, parsley

POTATOES: Paprika, herb seasoning mix, green bell pepper, mace, onion, parsley, caraway seed

SALADS: Italian seasoning, dill, fresh lemon juice, pepper, vinegar

SOUPS: Quick-Sip, Bragg Liquid Aminos, Jensen's Broth, dill, Vegit, Mrs. Dash, a pinch of dry mustard powder in bean soup, allspice, a small amount of vinegar in vegetable soup; peppercorns in skim milk chowders, bay leaves and parsley in pea soup

SQUASH: Cinnamon, ginger, mace, nutmeg, onion

Use The Herb Shaker—
Rather Than The Salt Shaker

You can use this herb magic in soups, vegetable dishes or with beans

1 Tbsp garlic powder
1 tsp each basil, mace, marjoram, onion powder, thyme, black pepper, parsley, sage and dill

Sprouting

Look at this day, for it is life. In its brief course lie all realities of existence. The splendor of action, the joy of growth, the bliss of love. For yesterday is only a dream and tomorrow but a vision. But today well lived, makes every yesterday a dream of happiness. And every tomorrow a vision of hope. Look well therefore to this day, for it is life.

From Sanskrit writings

Seeds are the core of life. Every seed contains the nutrients to nourish the growth of a future plant. A sprouted seed is a living chemistry lab. During sprouting the seed manufactures more vitamins, uses up some of the fat and carbohydrate calories and increases its fiber and water content.

By sprouting you wind up with a protein rich food which is higher in vitamins, lower in calories and fat, more easily digested and better assimilated than the original seed. Almost any bean, grain or seed will sprout. Choose organically grown seeds intended for eating, not garden seeds. I use sprouted wheat berries and sunflower seeds as a breakfast cereal or for sprout muffins. Radish, alfalfa, clover, mung beans, buckwheat and mustard sprouts are good for salads. Using sprouts is a tasty way to pack as many nutrients in as few calories as possible.

Technique

Listed below are ideal soaking times. Most seeds are forgiving, as far as soaking time is concerned. Just keep in mind that sprouts are alive and want to be handled with care. Don't drown them in water by soaking them too long. Rinsing sprouts cleanses and nourishes them. Do rinse them twice a day while they are sprouting and once a day while storing in the refrigerator. Drain all the water after rinsing as they need to breathe. Sprouts keep well if you store them in the refrigerator for about a week. Continue to rinse and drain them daily.

SEED	AMOUNT	SOAK TIME	HARVEST
Alfalfa	2 Tbsp per qt jar	5 hours	4-5 days
Clover	2 Tbsp per qt jar	5 hours	4-5 days
Fenugreek	⅕ of jar	7 hours	3-4 days
Sunflower	⅕ of jar	8 hours	2-3 days
Lentils	⅕ of jar	10 hours	2-3 days
Wheat	⅕ of jar	10 hours	2-4 days
Buckwheat	⅕ of jar	10 hours	3-4 days
Mung beans	⅕ of jar	12 hours	3-4 days

1. Wash seed and soak in water

2. Pour off soak water Rinse sprouts 3 times

3. Slant jar in drainer. Rinse twice a day, until water runs clear

CHAPTER 7
SAMPLE MENU PLAN

Let food be thy medicine

Hippocrates

To gain health and to lose weight, a menu plan is a good start. Here is a sample of our master menu plan for Sans Souci Health Resort. Make your own, simplifying it and checking your calendar to plan for times you eat out.

BREAKFAST	LUNCH	DINNER
Lemon Water	Zucchini Soup	Carrot Salad
Musli with	Stuffed Bible	Oven-baked Fish
Fruit	Bread Pockets	Potato-onion Casserole
Lemon Water	Split Pea Soup	Salad
Porridge	Pasta Primavera	Salmon Mousse
Fruit	Sprouts	Glazed Sweet Potatoes
Lemon Water	Calcium Booster	Greek Salad
Fresh Fruit	Soup	Fish in a Pouch
Whole Wheat	Fitness Swirl	Baked Stuffed Potato
Crepes	Jicama and Sprouts	Garnish
	Garnish	
Lemon Water	Carrot Soup	Cucumber Salad
French Toast	Bulgar Stir Fry	Seafood Divan
with Fruit	Tomatoes	Kashi
Lemon Water	Sprouted Bean	Salad
Fresh Fruit	Soup	Lehman's Rice Dish
Egg-white	Shrimp Crepe	Stuffed Mushrooms
Omelet	with Lemon Sauce	Veggies

SNACKS or DESERTS
Fresh veggies and fruit with dip, Swiss Rice Fruit Cream,
Carrot Apricot Souffle, Sans Souci Ice Cream,
Raw Apple Dessert

Change Your Eating Style

I can turn stumbling blocks into stepping stones, lemons into lemonade and challenges into triumphs

Letting go of old, ingrained habits can be a challenge for the most disciplined person. It takes three to four weeks to form a new habit. Start by empowering yourself with a new way of thinking, making a conscious decision to cultivate health. Here are 18 positive steps you can take to accomplish this change.

1. Plan a weekly menu and stick to it
2. Make a shopping list to control impulse shopping
3. Create a beautiful surrounding
4. Add a flower or candle on the table for joy
5. Eat only in one room, at the same table and chair
6. Eat only when hungry
7. Drink a large glass of water 5 minutes before each meal
8. Serve small individual portions
9. Do not serve family style
10. Slow your pace of eating
11. Take small bites, more bites per meal
12. Chew each mouthful slowly and carefully
13. Enjoy the food you eat
14. Lay fork or spoon down between each bite
15. Leave a little food on your plate at each meal
16. Leave the table immediately after you finish
17. Store leftover food immediately
18. Bring all senses into your eating pleasure: sight, smell, texture and taste

Please write me a card and tell me what worked for you.

Hunger Control

1. Avoid sugar and white flour

2. Eat whole grains and high fiber foods

3. Drink 6 to 8 glasses of water daily

4. Keep high calorie foods out of sight, out of mind

5. Reduce weight

6. Exercise

7. **R-E-L-A-X!**

Handling "Snack Attacks" The Sans Souci Way

The 6 "D's"

1. **D**elay. Hunger usually does not persist.
2. **D**o something else, like walking or calling a friend.
3. **D**rink lemon water, herbal tea, warm skim milk or soup.
4. **D**eep abdominal breathing, filling up on fresh air.
5. **D**o r - e - l - a - x, it reduces stress eating.
6. If all the above fails - **D**o not eat "what you can't wash."

CHAPTER 8
BASICS TO KEEP ON HAND

All nutritional analysis have been completed with the help of Nutritionist III, Version 7, University of Kentucky and Jean A.T. Pennington's book, *Food Values of Portions Commonly Used, 15th Edition.* Some of the recipes have approximated breakdown values. Throughout the book, the values following each recipe are for one serving.

Keeping healthy choices on hand makes it easier to stick to your plan. Here are some examples of what I find helpful.

LEMON WATER

The juice of 1 lemon added to four cups of water. I start every day, at home or at Sans Souci, with this refreshing drink. For variety you can add 1 cup of calcium-enriched fruit juices.

4 servings

Calories per serving: 4   Vitamin C: 8 mg

SOY MILK

Powdered soy milk, like Moo Soy Milk or Better Than Milk can enrich many a soup or casserole. It is available in regular and low fat.

Serving size: 8 oz
Calories per serving: 10   Fat: 2 g = 18% of total calories
Protein: 2 g   Sodium: 100 mg

FITNESS CHEESE

This tasty yogurt cheese is a must in my kitchen. It tastes better to me than cream cheese, yet has no fat. The fat content of cream cheese is—you guessed it, a high 90%! I use Fitness Cheese as a replacement for cream cheese or sour cream. It is good with chives on a baked potato or for bread spreads. Mixed with almond extract or other flavor enhancers it makes an excellent dip. It is well tolerated by people with lactose intolerance and is a whopper for calcium and protein.

Place 2 cups lowfat or nonfat yogurt in a cheese funnel. Cover with plastic wrap and place funnel in a glass or cup to drain. Refrigerate. Let drain for 1 to 3 days. The longer it drains, the more firm it becomes. **8 servings**

Calories per serving: 28
Fat: 0.10 g = 3% of total calories   Potassium: 145 mg
Cholesterol: 1 mg   Calcium: 113

SANS SOUCI MAYO

This tasty mayonnaise has only 1% fat by calories as opposed to the 99% fat of the store bought mayonnaise.

1 cup Fitness Cheese
1 tsp prepared mustard
1 Tbsp nonfat cucumber dressing
Fresh or dried dill to taste

Mix all ingredients well. Keep refrigerated. **9 Servings**

Calories per serving: 16
Fat: 0.05 g = 3% of total calories   Potassium: 77 mg
Cholesterol: 0.50 mg   Calcium: 59 mg

SAUERKRAUT

2 heads red or white cabbage, finely shredded; retain outer
    leaves
1 Tbsp herb seasoning mix
2 tsp garlic, chopped
2 tsp dill seed
2 tsp finely chopped dill weed
1 ripe apple, sliced

   In large bowl, mix all ingredients except apple slices. Press
in a one-gallon ceramic crock or glass jar. Place apple slices
and outer cabbage leaves over mixture. Seal the mixture by
filling a plastic ziplock bag with water and placing it on top.
Cover with clean towel. Store at room temperature 3 days.
Remove towel, plastic bag, cabbage leaves and apple slices.
Use as salad or steamed as side dish. Keep refrigerated.

10 servings

Calories per serving: 24   Potassium: 234 mg
Fat: 0.23 g = 8% of total calories   Calcium: 53 mg

SPLIT PEA PASTE

1 cup split peas
3 cups water
2 zucchini, cut in chunks
2 celery stalks, chopped
1 onion, chopped
4 garlic cloves, chopped
Bay leaf powder, Jensen's Broth, butter-flavor granules,
    herb seasoning mix, vegetable seasoning mix to taste
2 Tbsp soy milk, dry form

Soak peas in water for 2 to 3 hours. Add remaining ingredients, except soy milk. Cook for 10 minutes or until tender. Add milk. Blend in electric blender with enough cooking broth to form a paste. Serve as a bread spread with tomatoes and lettuce or add to soups and sauces as a thickener.

12 servings

Calories per serving: 70
Fat: 0.28 g = 4% of total calories   Calcium: 26 mg
Potassium: 290 mg   Fiber: 6.4 g

WHOLE WHEAT BREAD

3 cups water
¼ cup frozen apple juice concentrate, undiluted
1 package active dry yeast
5 cups whole wheat flour
1 cup oat bran
½ cup wheat germ
⅓ cup dried minced onion
3 Tbsp caraway seed
2 Tbsp low-sodium soy sauce or Quick-Sip

In large bowl, heat 1 cup water and apple juice until luke-warm. Add yeast and 1 cup whole wheat flour. Mix well, cover with towel and let stand in warm place for ½ hour. Add remaining ingredients and knead a few minutes. Cover with towel and let dough rise in a warm place until double in size. Divide dough in half and put in nonstick loaf pans. Cover with towel and let rise for an additional hour. Bake in preheated 375° oven for 50 minutes.

You can use all or part of the dough to form 1 inch wide bread strips. Brush with slightly beaten egg white. Add caraway seed and shredded nonfat cheese on top. Superb for dips. Bake at 375° for 30 minutes.

15 servings

Calories per serving: 181
Fat: 1.76 g = 8% of total calories   Calcium: 33 mg
Potassium: 299 mg   Fiber: 6.4 g

WHOLE WHEAT BAGEL

2 Tbsp active dry yeast
1 Tbsp honey
2 cups warm water

5 cups whole wheat flour
4 qt water

Dissolve yeast and honey in 2 cups warm water. Knead in flour, a half cup at a time, until dough is smooth. Knead 10 minutes. Let dough rise in warm place until double in size. Knead again for 5 minutes. Let rise once more until doubled. Divide into 18 pieces. Roll each into 1-inch rope. Form rings pinching ends together. In 6 qt. pan, bring 4 qt. water to a boil. Reduce to simmer. Cook 5 bagels at a time. When they rise to the surface continue cooking 5 minutes. Lift out; place on nonstick baking sheets. Bake at 350° for 30 minutes.   **Makes 18 bagels**

Calories per bagel: 120
Fat: 0.62 g = 4% of total calories

Potassium: 153 mg
Fiber: 4 g

VINEGAR

As a child in Rumania, I remember grandmother making vinegar from fresh apple cider. She lived in the country and ran an almost self-sufficient household, from homemade bread and preserves to vinegar.

Vinegar is simple to make. All you need is pure apple cider with no preservatives. Start with pouring apple cider into a jug or dark colored glass jar. Leave about ¼ empty to allow cider to expand during fermentation. Cover container with a cloth so cider can "breathe." Stretch cloth over jar top and tie it with string or elastic. Store in cool, dark place.   Fermentation takes from 4 to 6 months.

Taste vinegar after 4 months. If it is to your liking, strain it through a double layer of cheesecloth into bottles and seal with corks. If the vinegar is too weak, let it ferment longer, testing it every week for readiness. The jelly-like layer that forms on top of vinegar during fermentation is called "mother." You can save it to use as a starter for your next batch of vinegar. It will speed up fermentation. Enjoy your homemade vinegar for salad dressings and cooking.

Calories per Tbsp: 2

CHAPTER 9
APPETIZERS

In our fast-paced fast-food world, appetizers are often high in fat, salt and calories. The good news is that they don't have to be. Here are recipes for healthy appetizers that taste sinfully good. For people on a hectic schedule, these quick-to-fix appetizers also make good snacks or side dishes.

POTATO SKINS

Choose healthy looking potatoes without sprouts or green correlation. Mature potatoes can develop toxic levels of solanin especially around sprouts and in the greenish part of the skin.

2 medium potatoes, baked
2 Tbsp grated nonfat cheese
1 tsp caraway seed
½ tsp paprika

Cut potatoes in half lengthwise. Scoop out center of each half, leaving about ½-inch thickness. Sprinkle with cheese, caraway and paprika. Broil for 2 minutes or until crispy brown.

4 servings

Calories per serving: 95
Fat: 1.4 g = 13% of total calories   Sodium: 39 mg
Cholesterol: 5 mg   Fiber: 2 g

ONION RINGS

Patty Davidson, our manager, hung up the phone with a mischievous smile on her face. A family with two children wanted to come to the spa.   There was one stipulation; the 12-year-old daughter loved onion rings and asked if she *pleeease* could have onion rings at the spa. One of my favorite statements in my cooking classes is: "Any recipe can be de-junked!" Can I? Onion rings?? I am good at putting things off. I forgot the onion rings until weeks later when, on check-in day, an exuberant 12-year-old Sandy asked me, "Can I have onion rings?"   So off we went to the kitchen to experiment. Sandy liked our new concoction better than the deep fried "regular" onion rings. So did the rest of the family.

2 large onions
1 cup skim milk or soy milk
2 egg whites
1 cup whole wheat flour
1 Tbsp feta cheese, crumbled
1 tsp butter-flavor granules
Herb seasoning mix and vegetable seasoning mix to taste

Peel onions, cut in slices and break into rings; set aside. In electric blender, mix remaining ingredients until smooth. Spray a nonstick baking sheet with cooking spray. Dip onion rings in batter and place on preheated baking sheet. Bake at 400° for 30 minutes or until golden brown.   **6 servings**

Calories per serving: 169
Fat: 1.9 g = 9% of total calories   Potassium: 332 mg
Cholesterol: 5 mg   Fiber: 6 gm

BROCCOLI - CAULIFLOWER FLORETS

While checking Laura in for her week long stay at the Spa, she confessed, "The only vegetables I eat are deep fried." Laura's mother sent the 19-year-old college student to Sans Souci to help her go off the yo-yo cycle of weight gain and loss and learn to eat for health. The onion ring experience a few weeks earlier led to this delightful new way of preparing vegetables. Laura liked them and before long she learned to eat and enjoy the taste of steamed and crunchy raw vegetables.

1 cup skim milk or soy milk
2 egg whites
1 cup whole wheat flour
1 tsp butter-flavor granules
1 Tbsp feta cheese, crumbled
Herb seasoning mix and vegetable seasoning mix to taste
2 cups broccoli florets
2 cups cauliflower florets

In electric blender, mix first 6 ingredients until smooth. Spray a nonstick baking sheet with cooking spray. Dip florets in batter and place on baking sheet. Bake at 400° for 30 minutes or until golden brown. **6 servings**

Calories per serving: 117
Fat: 1.6 g = 12% of total calories
Cholesterol: 5 mg

Potassium: 381 mg
Calcium: 105 mg
Fiber: 5 g

NO FAT POTATO CHIPS

When I moved from Rumania to the U.S. and tried my very first potato chip I thought, "That's the cat's meow." They tasted wonderful and potatoes are good for you, right? So I ate potato chips - often! A few weeks and 5 pounds later I checked the label and found out that they had 52% fat. What a bummer! The potato is our lowest fat vegetable with only 1% fat and loaded with potassium, vitamin C and fiber. There must be a way, I thought, to enjoy the crispy taste of a potato chip without all the fat and salt.

Then I remembered that my grandmother used to cut potatoes in slices, season them with herbs and place them directly on the hot wood burning stove. Ten minutes later the wonderful aroma of herbs and crisped potatoes would bring us into the kitchen from our playground to enjoy our snack and her company. This slightly modified version of my grandmother's chips can be enjoyed as an appetizer with our vegetable dip or as a side dish for tuna burgers.

2 large potatoes
2 egg whites
Paprika, herb seasoning mix, vegetable seasoning mix, butter-
    flavored granules to taste
1 tsp Garlic Bread Sprinkle or Parmesan cheese, optional

Wash and cut potatoes in thin slices. Beat egg whites lightly, add seasonings except garlic. Dip potato slices in egg white mixture. Spray a nonstick baking sheet with cooking spray. Layer sliced potatoes like roof shingles on baking sheet. Sprinkle garlic on potatoes. Bake at 400° for 25 minutes or until crisp and lightly browned. **4 servings**

Calories per serving: 79
Fat: 0.3 g = 3% of total calories   Sodium: 41 mg
Cholesterol: 0.41 mg   Fiber: 2 gm

SEED SAUCE

⅓ cup sprouted sesame seed
⅔ cup lemon water
⅔ cup sprouted sunflower seed

In electric blender, blend sesame seed with half of lemon water until creamy. Add sunflower seed and remaining lemon water. Blend again until smooth and creamy. Use as dip with vegetables or fruit, on salads or as mayonnaise substitute for sandwiches.   **10 servings**

Calories per serving: 41
Protein: 2 g   Fat: 36 g = 78% of total calories

ANTS ON A LOG

4 celery stalks
2 Tbsp almond butter
1 Tbsp currants

Cut celery stalks in 3-inch pieces. Fill with almond butter and add 4 currants on each piece.   **6 servings**

Calories per serving: 39   Fat: 3 g = 69% of total calories
Protein: 1 g   Calcium: 26 mg

STUFFED VIDALIA ONIONS

 While visiting Sans Souci last summer, Karen, an alumna and now a friend, said, "Susie, somewhere I ate stuffed onions and liked them. I don't know the ingredients, but they surely tasted good. I love onions, do you think you could come up with a recipe?" Vidalia onions were in season. I had some cooked couscous from lunch in the refrigerator, and the rest seemed to fall in place. I tried the recipe later with regular onions and it didn't taste as good. Now I store Vidalia onions in a net or old stockings, which I hang in a cool place. They keep for 2 months.

4 small Vidalia onions
1 cup couscous, cooked
2 egg whites
½ cup split pea paste or frozen peas
½ cup nonfat grated cheese
½ cup chopped red bell peppers
1 Tbsp parsley flakes
Dill, vegetable seasoning mix, butter-flavor granules, herb
    seasoning mix to taste

 Peel onions, cut in half. Scoop out half of the inside; set aside. In medium bowl, mix remaining ingredients. Fill onion halves. Place on nonstick baking sheet. Bake at 400° for 30 minutes or until golden brown. Serve with Mustard Sauce.

8 servings

Calories per serving: 105   Cholesterol: 8 mg
Fat: 7.35 g = 8% of total calories Fiber: 3 g

Mustard Sauce

1/4 cup water
2 Tbsp prepared mustard

 In saucepan, combine ingredients; mix well. Heat to a low boil. Serve over Stuffed Vidalia Onions and other recipes.

STUFFED MUSHROOMS

This simple recipe is a winner at any party. Low in calories, stuffed mushrooms make a tasty bite-size finger food. Because of their high water content, mushrooms become soggy when washed in water. To avoid this simply wipe them clean with a damp paper towel.

16 medium mushroom caps
1 cup Fitness Cheese or lowfat cottage cheese
¼ cup non-fat grated cheese or feta cheese, crumbled
¼ cup whole wheat breadcrumbs
2 egg whites, slightly beaten
1 Tbsp onion flakes
1 Tbsp chopped fresh parsley
Dill, tarragon, vegetable seasoning mix, herb seasoning mix,
      butter-flavor granules to taste

Clean mushroom caps with a damp paper towel; set aside. In medium bowl, combine remaining ingredients. Stuff mushrooms with mixture. Place on nonstick baking sheet. Bake at 400° for 25 minutes. Serve warm on small lettuce leaf. If you have left-over mixture, form small balls, roll them in whole wheat breadcrumbs. Bake at 400° for 25 minutes. **8 servings**

Calories per serving: 52   Cholesterol: 6.5
Fat: 1 g = 17% of total calories   Calcium: 65 mg

BROILED MUSHROOMS

Easy and fun, I will eat them as lunch with a big salad and whole wheat crackers. They make a good side dish for almost any dinner. You can use the mushroom stems for soups or other vegetable dishes.

15 medium mushroom caps
2 Tbsp grated nonfat cheese
1 tsp paprika

Clean mushroom caps with wet paper towel. Sprinkle with cheese and paprika. Broil for 5 minutes or until golden brown.

5 servings

Calories per serving: 17.3   Cholesterol: 2.7 mg
Fat: 0.35 g = 20%   Potassium: 120 mg

HUMMUS

An all-time favorite at parties, hummus makes a tasty dip for a vegetable platter. On toasted Bible Bread or whole wheat pita bread, hummus provides a complete protein. Make colorful tidbits by spreading hummus on melba toast, top with chopped up red bell peppers and scallions. You can use it as a spread for small sandwiches which you can decorate with red radish slices and parsley.

2 cups cooked chick-peas
½ cup lemon juice
⅓ cup Tahini
2 cloves garlic, pressed
1 Tbsp low-sodium soy sauce or Bragg Liquid Aminos

In electric blender, mix all ingredients until smooth.

6 servings

Calories per serving: 126   Potassium: 306 mg
Fat: 3.6 g = 26% of total calories Calcium: 82 mg

TARAMA

Maria, an out-of-town friend, came for an unexpected, much enjoyed visit. She refused to let me shop for food and instead suggested we try something new. We found the necessary ingredients in my pantry. This Greek dip goes well with whole grain rye or Bible Bread strips.

2 medium boiled potatoes, cut in cubes
1 can (3¾ oz) water-packed sardines, drained
½ cup nonfat yogurt
2 Tbsp lemon juice
2 Tbsp minced onions
1 Tbsp chopped fresh parsley

In electric blender, blend first 4 ingredients until smooth. Stir in onions and parsley. **6 servings**

Calories per serving: 72   Cholesterol: 6 mg
Fat: 0.45 g = 6% of total calories   Potassium: 274 mg

STUFFED CHERRY TOMATOES

They are easy to make and will delight you and your guests without adding any fat to your diet. Instead of, or in addition to tomato you can use 2-inch cut celery or French endive leaves.

1 cup Fitness Cheese
1 tsp finely chopped fresh parsley
1 tsp caraway seed
1 tsp paprika
Herb seasoning mix and vegetable seasoning mix to taste
15 cherry tomatoes

In small bowl, combine first 5 ingredients. Cut off tops of tomatoes. Scoop out centers with melon scoop. Stuff tomatoes with mixture. **5 servings**

Calories per serving: 47   Cholesterol: 2.8 mg
Fat: 1 g = 19% of total calories   Calcium: 91 mg

FRUIT DIP WITH STRAWBERRIES

You can use this tasty dip with any fruit of your choice.

½ cup Fitness Cheese
½ cup nonfat yogurt
½ tsp maple extract or cinnamon
Honey or barley extract to sweeten
2 lb strawberries, washed and cut in half

In small bowl, combine all ingredients, except strawberries. Serve with fruit.   **6 servings**

Calories per serving: 81
Fat: 0.5 g = 6% of total calories   Calcium: 93 mg
Cholesterol: 1 mg   Fiber: 4 g

VEGETABLE DIP

½ cup Fitness Cheese
½ cup nonfat yogurt
1 Tbsp nonfat cucumber dressing
Dill, herb seasoning mix, vegetable seasoning mix to taste

In small bowl, combine all ingredients. Serve with cut up raw vegetables.   **8 servings**

Calories per serving: 20   Cholesterol: 1 mg
Fat: 0.24 g = 11% total calories   Calcium: 28 mg

CUCUMBER SANDWICHES WITH MINT

Once or twice a week we have an afternoon tea party at Sans Souci. It is fun to sit around a small table and pass the cucumber sandwiches. Usually our tea party is on the day when we have cooking class. The fresh whole wheat bread we baked in class does not need toasting. Both bagels and bread make good sandwiches.

1 cup Fitness Cheese
1 tsp caraway seed
½ tsp paprika
Herb seasoning mix and vegetable seasoning mix to taste
3 whole wheat bagels
1 small cucumber, sliced
Fresh mint leaves

Mix first 4 ingredients. Slice bagels in thirds and toast. Cut in 2-inch pieces. Spread mixture on bagels. Top with cucumber and mint leaves.   **8 servings**

Calories per serving: 49   Potassium: 142 mg
Fat: 0.86 g = 16% total calories   Calcium: 66 mg
Cholesterol: 2 mg   Sodium: 62 mg

GLAZED SHRIMP

1 Tbsp gelatin
1 cup vegetable stock
Herb seasoning mix and hot sauce to taste
1 lb boiled and cleaned shrimp

Dissolve gelatin in warm vegetable stock. Season and chill until glaze thickens somewhat. Cut shrimp lengthwise down the center and spear on picks. Dip in glaze. When partly set, dip again. Chill and serve cold.   **8 servings**

Calories per serving: 58   Fat: 0.61 g = 9.5% of total calories
Protein: 12.3 g   Cholesterol: 111 mg

VEGETABLE SPREAD FOR BAGELS

I have tried to convince local bagel shops to keep this no fat bagel spread in their stores as an option to the 90% fat cream cheese spread but haven't yet succeeded. I will try again, but I need your help. As consumers, we have an awesome power. Ask for low fat spreads. If more of us request healthy, lowfat food choices, it is more likely they will be provided. Our food industry has changed already because the demand for low fat, healthy choices has increased.

1 cup Fitness Cheese
½ small red bell pepper, chopped
1 celery stalk with leaves, chopped
1 scallion, chopped
Herb seasoning mix and vegetable seasoning mix to taste

In mixing bowl, combine all ingredients. Serve with bagels or whole wheat crackers. **6 servings**

Calories per serving: 26
Fat: 0.63 g = 4% of total calories
Cholesterol: 0.66 mg

Potassium: 70 mg
Calcium: 43 mg
Sodium: 32 mg

STUFFED BEETS

6 small cooked beets
3 hard-cooked egg whites, chopped
2 Tbsp nonfat mayonnaise
½ tsp each tarragon, parsley and chives
1 tsp prepared horseradish

Peel beets; cut in half. Hollow slightly. Mix remaining ingredients and fill the hollowed beets. Garnish with parsley.
6 servings

Calories per serving: 58
Fat: 0.4 g = 6% of total calories

Cholesterol: 1 mg
Potassium: 196 mg

CHAPTER 10
BREAKFASTS

SPROUT BREAKFAST

This chewy breakfast is one of our healthiest choices at the Spa and better liked than I thought it would be. You can substitute spelt for wheat and crispy rice cereal for granola. If fresh raspberries are not available, you can use frozen berries, thawed.

½ cup sprouted wheat berries
¼ cup sprouted sunflower seed
½ cup raspberries
2 Tbsp Sans Souci Granola
1 cup skim milk or soy milk

In 2 serving bowls, combine sprouts. Top with granola and fruit. Add milk. Chew well. **2 servings**

Calories per serving: 144
Fat: 4 g = 24% of total calories
Cholesterol: 2 mg

Potassium: 130 mg
Calcium: 168 mg
Fiber: 4 gm

MUSLI

This delightful breakfast from Switzerland can easily be changed to fit your taste preference. If you don't have sprouted wheat berries you can use oats or rolled barley. Instead of sunflower seeds try chopped hazelnuts or walnuts. I grew up on Musli and am very grateful to my mother for providing such a wholesome breakfast or snack for us on a regular basis. Have fun experimenting and see which you like best.

1½ cup lowfat yogurt
½ cup rolled oats
3 Tbsp sprouted wheat berries
2 Tbsp sprouted sunflower seed
1 Tbsp wheat germ
1 Tbsp flax seeds
1 Tbsp raisins or currants
1 Tbsp honey
1 apple, grated
3 Tbsp lemon juice

In medium bowl, combine all ingredients except apple and lemon juice. Cover grated apples with lemon juice to prevent them from turning brown. Mix apple into musli mixture. Garnish with fresh fruit. **4 servings**

Calories per serving: 198
Fat: 2 g = 13% of total calories
Cholesterol: 11 mg
Potassium: 628 mg

Calcium: 332 mg
Sodium: 13 mg
Fiber: 4 g

SANS SOUCI GRANOLA

3 cups rolled oats
1 cup wheat germ
1 cup roasted soy beans
½ cup oat bran
½ cup wheat bran
½ cup sunflower seed
½ cup flax seed
½ cup dry milk
½ cup almonds, sliced
1 tsp cinnamon
¼ cup vegetable oil
⅓ cup honey

In large mixing bowl, combine all ingredients except oil and honey. Place in nonstick baking sheet, distributing evenly. Mix oil and honey in small pan and heat.   Pour over dry mixture. Bake at 325° for 15 minutes or until lightly browned and crisp, mixing occasionally.   **20 servings**

Calories per serving: 58
Protein: 9 g   Potassium: 329 mg
Fat: 10 g = 41% of total calories   Sodium: 25 g
Cholesterol: 0.3 mg   Fiber: 3 g

HOT OAT BRAN CEREAL

1 cup water
⅓ cup oat bran
1 Tbsp wheat bran
2 Tbsp raisins
½ cup soy milk or skim milk

In small pan, combine water, oat and wheat bran. Cook 3 minutes. Add raisins. Serve with milk.   **2 servings**

Calories per serving: 98   Calcium: 21 mg
Fat: 2 g = 16% of total calories   Sodium: 13 mg
Potassium: 286 mg   Fiber: 4 g

EGG WHITE OMELETTE

½ red bell pepper, diced
1 scallion, chopped
4 mushrooms, sliced
Parsley, vegetable seasoning mix, herb seasoning mix, butter-
    flavored granules to taste
4 egg whites or the equivalent in powdered egg whites
2 Tbsp lowfat cottage cheese

Steam vegetables 5 minutes. Add seasonings. In medium bowl, beat egg whites; stir in vegetables and cottage cheese. Spray 8-inch nonstick skillet with cooking spray. Spoon omelette mixture in heated skillet. Cook on each side for 5 minutes or until done.   **2 servings**

Calories per serving: 51   Cholesterol: 0.63 mg
Protein: 9 g   Potassium: 191 mg
Fat: 0.23 g = 4% of total calories   Calcium: 19 mg

PORRIDGE

1 cup skim milk
½ cup rolled oats
1 Tbsp sunflower seed
1 Tbsp thawed and undiluted apple juice concentrate
1 tsp currants
Dash cinnamon
1 banana, sliced

In small pan, combine all ingredients, except banana. Cook 1 or 2 minutes. Top with banana.   **2 servings**

Calories per serving: 165
Fat: 4 g = 21% of total calories   Calcium: 361 mg
Cholesterol: 3 mg   Sodium: 62 mg
Potassium: 686 mg   Fiber: 3 g

CREPES SUZETTE

1 cup skim milk
¾ cup whole wheat flour
2 egg whites
1 Tbsp lemon peel
1 tsp butter-flavor granules

   In electric blender, blend all ingredients until smooth. Spray an 8-inch pan with cooking spray, then heat. Add about ¼ cup batter to the pan, swirling the batter so it covers the bottom of the pan. Cook on both sides until lightly browned. Makes about 6 crepes.

Filling

2 cups Fitness Cheese
1 cup fresh or frozen raspberries
2 Tbsp honey
Fresh fruit
Mint leaves

   In medium bowl, combine cheese, berries and honey. Add 2 Tbsp filling to each crepe, roll crepes. Garnish with fruit and mint leaves. Serve immediately.   **6 servings**

Calories per serving: 167
Fat: 0.84 g = 4.5% of total calories   Calcium: 218 mg
Cholesterol: 2 mg   Sodium: 99 g
Potassium: 406 mg   Fiber: 4 g

FITNESS BLINTZES

1 cup Fitness Cheese
1 small banana
1 Tbsp honey
1 tsp vanilla
Pinch of cinnamon
3 egg whites
6 whole wheat crepes, see Crepes Suzette
1 cup frozen berries

In electric blender, blend first 5 ingredients until smooth. Beat egg whites until stiff peaks form. Fold egg whites into cheese mixture. Place 3 Tbsp of the blintz filling into each crepe. Roll crepes and place on a nonstick baking pan. Cover with foil. Bake at 350° for 20 minutes. Heat berries and spoon over crepes. **6 servings**

Calories per serving: 197
Fat: 0.9 g = 4% of total calories
Cholesterol: 3 mg

Potassium: 566 mg
Calcium: 296 mg
Fiber: 4 mg

FRENCH TOAST

4 egg whites
¼ cup skim milk or soy milk
Vanilla and cinnamon to taste
2 whole wheat bagels
6 oz fatfree fruit yogurt

In medium bowl, whisk egg whites, milk, vanilla and cinnamon. Slice bagel in thirds. Soak each slice in egg white mixture for one minute. Heat a nonstick pan and spray with cooking spray. Cook over medium heat on each side until golden brown. Top with yogurt. **4 servings**

Calories per serving: 97
Fat: 0.39 g = 4% of total calories
Cholesterol: 0.25
Potassium: 157 mg

Calcium: 51 mg
Sodium: 68 mg
Fiber: 2 mg

POLENTA - MAMALIGA

2 cups water
½ cup whole grain yellow cornmeal
1 tsp butter-flavor granules
1 cup skim milk

In medium saucepan, bring water to a boil. Stir in cornmeal and butter-flavor granules. Simmer for 10 minutes, stirring frequently. Serve with skim milk. **2 servings**

Calories per serving: 102   Calcium: 115 mg
Fat: 1 g = 9% of total calories   Fiber: 4 g

BLUEBERRY MUFFINS

1 cup whole wheat pastry flour
1 cup oat bran
1 cup wheat germ
¼ cup sunflower seed
1 tsp baking powder
1 tsp baking soda
1 cup nonfat milk
½ cup nonfat yogurt
¼ cup frozen apple juice concentrate, thawed and undiluted
1 Tbsp vanilla
4 egg whites
1 package (12 oz) frozen blueberries, thawed

In large bowl, mix well all ingredients except egg whites and blueberries. Beat egg whites until stiff peaks form, fold into batter, then fold in the frozen blueberries. Pour batter into nonstick muffin pans. Bake at 400° for 30 minutes.
Makes 25 muffins

Calories per muffin: 73   Cholesterol: 0.24 mg
Fat: 1.7 g = 19% of total calories   Fiber: 2 mg

CHAPTER 11
SALADS AND DRESSINGS

SANS SOUCI VINAIGRETTE DRESSING

This dressing is easy to make and keeps refrigerated for a month. For variety in taste and texture, you can mix it with commercial fatfree dressings.

1 cup apple cider vinegar
1 cup lemon juice
1½ cups water
⅓ cup frozen apple juice concentrate, undiluted
2 cloves garlic, crushed
Dill, onion powder, fines herbs, vegetable seasoning mix, herb
    seasoning mix, Italian seasoning, thyme to taste

In mixing bowl or large jar combine all ingredients; mix well.
Refrigerate.   **26 servings**

Calories per serving: 21   Potassium: 70.5 mg
Fat: 0.08 g = 3% of total calories   Sodium: 5 mg

NUTTY DELIGHT

2 cups water
1 cup soaked sunflower seed or pine nuts
½ cup soaked almonds
½ lemon, juiced
2 cloves garlic
3 Tbsp Quick-Sip or Bragg Liquid Aminos
2 Tbsp chopped fresh parsley
Pinch oregano

In electric blender, blend all ingredients until smooth. Serve as a salad dressing or with steamed vegetables. **10 servings**

Calories per serving: 62
Protein: 2.4 g   Fat: 4.9 g = 71% of total calories

EUROPEAN FANTASY DRESSING

1 red bell pepper, cubed
1 cup water
2 Tbsp flax seed
2 Tbsp sunflower seed
1 scallion
Herb seasoning mix and vegetable seasoning mix to taste

In electric blender, blend all ingredients until smooth. Refrigerate for 30 minutes to allow sauce to thicken. Serve as a salad dressing.   **6 servings**

Calories per serving: 28   Potassium: 73 mg
Fat: 1.6 g = 53% of total calories   Calcium: 19 mg

CLEANSING SALAD

¼ head cabbage, chopped
1 apple, peeled and diced
1 orange, peeled and sectioned
1 stalk of celery, chopped
1 carrot, grated
⅓ cup currants, soaked in water
⅓ cup sprouted sunflower seed
¼ cup Sans Souci Vinaigrette Dressing
½ cup alfalfa sprouts

Layer ingredients in salad bowl beginning with cabbage, apple, orange, celery, carrot, currants, sunflower sprouts and dressing. Garnish with sprouts. **6 servings**

Calories per serving: 61 mg
Protein: 1.39 g   Cholesterol: 0.67 mg
Fat: 2 g = 32% of total calories   Fiber: 3 g

ENDIVE SALAD

1 lb Belgian endive
1 apple, grated
⅓ cup chopped walnuts or sprouted sunflower seed
¼ cup currants, soaked in water
¼ cup lowfat celery seed dressing

Wash and separate endive leaves, break leaves into bite size pieces. Toss with remaining ingredients. **4 servings**

Calories per serving: 87
Fat: 2.3 g = 24% of total calories   Potassium: 500 mg
Cholesterol: 1 mg   Fiber: 2

SILLY - DILLY CUKES

3 cucumbers, peeled and cut into 1/2-inch cubes
2 scallions, chopped
½ cup nonfat yogurt
Paprika and dill to taste

In small bowl, combine all ingredients. Garnish with parsley.

3 servings

Calories per serving: 31
Fat: 0.3 g = 9% of total calories

Cholesterol: 0.67 mg
Calcium: 93 mg

RUMANIAN EGGPLANT SALAD

2 medium eggplants
2 Tbsp vinegar
1 Tbsp seed sauce or Tahini
Butter-flavor granules, vegetable seasoning mix, herb
seasoning mix, dill, garlic powder to taste
3 scallions, chopped

Poke holes in eggplants and microwave until soft to touch, about 30 minutes. Cut eggplant lengthwise and spoon insides into blender. Add remaining ingredients except scallions. Blend until smooth. Spoon mixture into bowl. Mix in scallions. Serve as a dip, as a salad or as a bread spread with tomatoes.

3 servings

Calories per serving: 38
Fat: 0.45 g = 9% of total calories
Potassium: 288 mg

Calcium: 22 mg
Sodium: 4 mg
Fiber: 3 g

COLE SLAW

2 cups shredded cabbage
½ shredded carrot
1 medium onion, finely chopped
1 Tbsp crushed juniper berries
1 Tbsp caraway seed or celery seed
½ cup Sans Souci Vinaigrette Dressing

In medium bowl, mix all ingredients well. Refrigerate for several hours. **6 servings**

Calories per serving: 18
Fat: 0.2 g = 10% of total calories

Potassium: 128 mg
Calcium: 25 mg

PARSNIP SALAD

2 cups finely grated parsnips
½ cup chopped red bell pepper
¼ cup minced parsley
½ cup water
½ cup soaked almonds
2 Tbsp Quick-Sip or Bragg Liquid Aminos
1 clove garlic

In medium bowl, combine first 3 ingredients. Set aside. In electric blender, blend remaining ingredients until smooth. Add to parsnip mixture. **6 servings**

Calories per serving: 77
Fat: 2.8 g = 33% of total calories

Potassium: 258 mg
Fiber: 3.3 g

WHITE CORN SALAD

2 cups fresh white corn kernels
1 cup chopped red bell pepper
2 scallions, chopped
¼ cup minced parsley
2 Tbsp water
2 Tbsp Quick-Sip or Bragg Liquid Aminos
2 Tbsp yellow corn
2 tsp fresh dill

In medium bowl, combine first 4 ingredients. Set aside. In electric blender, blend remaining ingredients. Pour over corn mixture. **6 servings**

Calories per serving: 23   Calcium: 16.6 mg
Fat: 0.28 g = 11% of total calories   Fiber: 1.7 g

CELERY ROOT SALAD

1 large celery root, grated
1 carrot, grated
1 green apple, grated
3 Tbsp reduced calorie celery seed dressing
2 Tbsp crushed walnuts or toasted almond slivers
2 Tbsp currants, soaked in water

In medium bowl, combine all ingredients. Serve garnished with parsley. **4 servings**

Calories per serving: 62   Calcium: 16 mg
Fat: 2.2 g = 32% of total calories   Sodium: 13 mg
Potassium: 188 mg   Fiber: 3 g

PINEAPPLE WALDORF SALAD

2 apples, unpeeled, diced
1 Tbsp lemon juice
½ cup diced celery
½ cup ripe pineapple chunks
½ cup lowfat celery seed dressing
2 Tbsp currants, soaked in water
10 leaves salad greens
¼ cup pecan halves

In medium bowl, combine apples with lemon juice. Add remaining ingredients except salad greens and nuts. Mix lightly. Serve on salad greens and garnish with the nuts.

4 servings

Calories per serving: 106
Fat: 4.6 g = 39% of total calories
Potassium: 246 mg

Calcium: 28 mg
Sodium: 6.3 mg
Fiber: 2.9 g

HERBED POTATO SALAD

½ cup nonfat Ranch dressing
1 Tbsp Dijon mustard
6 medium potatoes, boiled and sliced
1 red onion, sliced
1 small red bell pepper, sliced
1 Tbsp each chopped fresh dill, parsley and chives

In large bowl, mix dressing and mustard. Combine with remaining ingredients. Serve as side dish. For a complete meal you can add 2 sliced hard-cooked egg whites.

6 servings

Calories per serving: 135
Fat: 0.38 g = 3% of total calories

Calcium: 31 mg
Fiber: 2.7 g

CARROT - PINEAPPLE SALAD

1 can (8 oz) crushed pineapple with the juice
⅓ cup currants or raisins, soaked in water for 2 hours
1 lemon, juiced
4 carrots
½ cup sprouted sunflower seed

In large bowl combine pineapple, currants and lemon juice. Grate carrots and immediately add to pineapple mixture. Top with sunflower seeds.   **6 servings**

Calories per serving: 68   Potassium: 200 mg
Fat: 0.24 g = 3% of total calories   Fiber: 3 g

CHAPTER 12
SOUPS

CARROT SOUP

My mother made this soup regularly as I grew up back in Rumania. I loved it then and I love it now. Replacing the salt and cream with herbs and soy milk hasn't diminished the wonderful taste.

3 carrots, sliced
2 large potatoes, cubed
1 small onion, chopped
4 cups water
Dill, Jensen's Broth, herb seasoning mix, butter-flavor
        granules to taste
2 Tbsp soy milk powder

In large pan, combine all ingredients, except milk powder. Cook for 10 minutes. In electric blender, blend carrot mixture and milk powder until smooth. Serve garnished with yogurt and parsley.   **5 servings**

Calories per serving: 78   Calcium: 52 m
Fat: 0.22 g = 2% of total calories   Sodium: 25 mg
Potassium: 262 mg   Fiber: 3 g

CALCIUM BOOSTER SOUP

Because I have difficulty digesting milk and milk products I have developed this soup to provide a high calcium food for those of us with lactose intolerance. Combining a grain and a legume provides a complete protein. I use frozen chopped greens, they are available year round.

1 cup dried split peas
4 cups water
1 cup chopped mustard greens
1 cup chopped turnip greens
1 cup chopped collard greens or kale
1 cup fresh or frozen corn
1 large sweet potato, cubed
1 carrot, cut in chunks
1 onion, peeled and cut in chunks
4 cloves garlic, minced
2 Tbsp butter-flavor granules
2 Tbsp Jensen's Broth powder
Tarragon, dill, vegetable seasoning mix, herb seasoning mix,
	Quick-Sip to taste
2 cups soy milk
1 Tbsp finely chopped fresh parsley
Nonfat yogurt for garnish

Soak peas for 10 hours in water. Discard soaking water. Add 4 cups fresh water and remaining ingredients, except soy milk, parsley and yogurt. Cook for 10 minutes or until tender. In food processor, combine pea mixture with milk and parsley; blend until smooth. Reheat and garnish with one teaspoon yogurt. **10 servings**

Calories per serving: 130
Fat: 1.3 g = 9% of total calories
Potassium: 459 mg

Calcium: 166 mg
Sodium: 26
Fiber: 3 g

SANS SOUCI VEGETABLE SOUP

To prevent oxidation and loss of nutrients, immediately place cut vegetables in a large pan with water. Cover the pan and cook as directed below. I keep this soup in the refrigerator and/or freezer as a back-up for snack attacks. It tastes wonderful, is low in calories and loaded with nutrients. If there is leftover cooked rice, I add it to the soup for a satisfying lunch. For variety you can add or substitute different vegetables.

¼ head of cabbage, diced
1 onion, diced
4 garlic cloves, minced
2 stalks of celery, sliced
2 carrots, sliced
1 cup cauliflower florets
1 large sweet potato, cubed
1 cup Brussels sprouts, quartered
8 asparagus spears, cut in 1-inch pieces
1 cup chopped collard greens or spinach
5 cups water
Dill, Jensen's Broth, Quick-Sip, vegetable seasoning mix, herb
    seasoning mix, butter-flavor granules to taste
1 cup fresh corn
1 cup green peas, fresh or frozen
1 cup no salt V8 juice
2 Tbsp each chopped fresh parsley and watercress

In large pan, combine first 11 ingredients. Cover and simmer for 8 minutes. Add remaining ingredients. Reheat and serve. **10 servings**

Calories per serving: 68   Calcium: 39 mg
Fat: 0.47 g = 6% of total calories   Sodium: 33 mg
Potassium: 105 mg   Fiber: 4 gm

GREEN BEAN SOUP

Summertime, when the green beans grow abundantly in our vegetable garden, I prepare this soup every week. It has a rich taste, is filling and high in nutrients. Serve with whole wheat pretzel.

1 lb green beans, cut in 2-inch pieces
1 large sweet potato, cubed
1 carrot, sliced
1 onion, diced
4 cups of water
3 bay leaves
1 Tbsp arrowroot flour or corn starch
2 Tbsp soy milk powder
2 Tbsp vinegar
2 Tbsp each Jensen's Broth and Quick-Sip
Vegetable seasoning mix, butter-flavor granules, Tabasco
    to taste

In large pan, combine first 6 ingredients. Bring to a boil and simmer 15 minutes. In small bowl, mix flour with 3 Tbsp cold water until smooth. Add to soup, stirring well. Remove soup from heat. Add remaining ingredients. Remove bay leaves.

6 servings

Calories per serving: 73   Potassium: 399 mg
Fat: 0.34 g = 4% of total calories   Sodium: 18 mg
Cholesterol: 0.25 mg   Fiber: 3 g

ZUCCHINI SOUP

4 zucchini, sliced
1 large sweet potato, cubed
1 onion, sliced
2 cloves garlic, sliced
3 cups Jensen's Broth or water
Rosemary, dill, herb seasoning mix, Jensen's Broth,
    Quick-Sip to taste
1 tsp butter-flavor granules
2 Tbsp soy milk powder

   In large pan, combine all ingredients except milk powder.
Bring to a boil and simmer for 10 minutes. Add milk powder. In
electric blender blend all ingredients until smooth. Garnish with
thin slice of zucchini.   **6 servings**

Calories per serving: 41   Cholesterol: 0.25 mg
Fat: .12 g = 3% of total calories   Fiber: 2 g

CHILLED FRUIT SOUP

3 cups frozen cantaloupe balls or any other frozen fruit
3 cups soy milk
Barley malt, cinnamon and nutmeg to taste

   In electric blender, blend all ingredients until smooth.
Garnish with fresh mint leaf, serve immediately.   **4 servings**

Calories per serving: 101   Potassium: 515 mg
Protein: 5.8 g   Calcium: 40 mg
Fat: 3.9 g = 35% of total calories   Sodium: 30 mg

SPROUTED BEAN SOUP

You can buy the sprouted bean medley in any health food store. Because the beans are sprouted they are higher in nutrients and easier to cook. I like the packages with the 5 different beans. Serve with toasted whole wheat bagel or bran muffin.

1 package sprouted bean medley
5 cups water or Jensen's Broth
1 cup mushrooms, sliced
1 tomato, diced
1 carrot, sliced
½ cup fresh or frozen corn
1 cup kale, chopped
1 onion, diced
3 cloves garlic, crushed
Bay leaf powder, dill, Jensen's Broth, Tabasco, herb seasoning
     mix to taste
1 tsp herb vinegar

Soak bean medley in water for 8 hours. Boil for 6 minutes. Add remaining ingredients, except vinegar. Boil an additional 6 minutes. Add vinegar.   **6 servings**

Calories per serving: 59   Calcium: 43 mg
Fat: 0.72 g = 11% of total calories   Sodium: 24 mg
Potassium: 301 mg   Fiber: 3 g

LENTIL SOUP

If you serve this soup with whole wheat bread or any other grain, it provides a complete protein making meat unnecessary for good nutrition. For variety you can replace the lentils with split peas.

2 cups lentils
6 cups water
5 cups Jensen's Broth
4 garlic cloves, crushed
1 large onion, chopped
1 carrot, sliced
1 cup chopped celery
1 zucchini, sliced
1 Tbsp butter-flavor granules
2 Tbsp soy milk powder
Herb seasoning mix, dill, rosemary, Bragg Liquid Aminos, freshly ground pepper to taste

Soak lentils in 6 cups water for 10 hours. Discard soaking water. Add remaining ingredients except milk and herbs. Cook 15 minutes or until tender. Add herbs and soy milk, reheat, serve. Garnish with 1 tsp nonfat yogurt. **6 servings**

Calories per serving: 135
Fat: 1.24 g = 8% of total calories
Potassium: 583 mg

Calcium: 53 mg
Sodium: 39 mg
Fiber: 6 g

VEGETARIAN CHILI

You will not miss the meat in this delicious recipe. The combination of bean and corn provides a complete protein. For variety you can replace the corn with brown rice or soaked bulgur wheat. Chili improves its taste by sitting a few hours or overnight. It is an ideal dish to prepare before guests arrive.

3 cups tomato sauce, no salt added
2 tomatoes, chopped
2 medium onions, chopped
2 large cloves garlic, minced
1 stalk celery, chopped
1 green bell or yellow bell pepper, chopped
1 Tbsp chopped hot peppers , canned
2 Tbsp each, mild chili powder, ground cumin, brown sugar
    and Jensen's Broth powder
¼ tsp each coriander, cloves, allspice, oregano and basil
1 cup fresh or frozen white corn
2 cups cooked kidney or pinto beans

In large pan, combine all ingredients, except corn and beans. Cook for 10 to 15 minutes. Add beans and corn. Bring to a boil and remove from heat. **5 servings**

Calories per serving: 92   Calcium: 56 mg
Fat: 0.53 g = 5% of total calories Sodium: 22 mg
Potassium: 417 mg   Fiber: 2 g

COLD CUCUMBER SOUP

1 cup nonfat yogurt
1 garlic clove
1 Tbsp tarragon vinegar
½ tsp grated lemon peel
Dill and herb seasoning mix to taste
½ cup Jensen's Broth, chilled
1 cucumber, peeled and shredded
2 Tbsp chopped fresh parsley

In electric blender, combine first 4 ingredients and seasonings. Blend until garlic is well blended. Add broth, blend until smooth. In medium bowl, combine cucumber, yogurt mixture and parsley. Cover and chill 1 hour. Garnish with cucumber slice. **3 servings**

Calories per serving: 66
Fat: 1.4 g = 19% of total calories
Cholesterol: 7 g

Potassium: 532 mg
Calcium: 253 mg
Sodium: 85 mg

GAZPACHO

This no-cook "sun cooked" soup with garden fresh vegetables is refreshing and always a hit with spa guests. It keeps well for a day or two in the refrigerator.

2 cups tomato juice or V8, salt-free
3 Tbsp vinegar
1 clove garlic, crushed
Butter-flavor granules, pepper, Tabasco to taste
2 ripe tomatoes, chopped
1 cucumber, chopped
1 green bell pepper, seeded and chopped
1 onion, diced

In electric blender, combine first 4 ingredients and ½ of all vegetables. Blend until smooth. Garnish with the remaining half of chopped vegetables.   **5 servings**

Calories per serving: 60   Calcium: 33 mg
Fat: .42 g = 6% of total calories   Sodium: 22 mg
Potassium: 525 mg   Fiber: 4 g

CHAPTER 13
VEGETARIAN ENTREES

LEHMAN'S RICE DISH

Mr. Lehman was a honorary member of the national ski patrol in Rumania. As an avid mountain climber, close to 80 years old, he still marked the trails. When I became a member of the national ski patrol, I admired his stamina and resistance to the icy winter storms during our mountain rescue training. I found out he ate a simple diet of grains and vegetables. We became friends and it is to a large extent due to him that I became a vegetarian. This was his favorite dish, which he ate almost every day. I have glamorized it with almonds, sprouts and seasonings. Thank you, Mr. Lehman.

1 cup brown rice	1 cup green peas
¼ cup wild rice	½ cup raisins, soaked
3½ cups water	½ cup sunflower seed, soaked
1 medium onion, chopped	¼ cup toasted almond slivers
2 carrots, grated	1 Tbsp chopped fresh parsley

Jensen's Broth, herb seasoning mix, butter-flavor granules, vegetable seasoning mix to taste

In large pan, wash rice well. Soak in water for 10 hours, add onion, boil for 5 minutes. Add carrots, continue cooking 4 minutes. Remove from heat. Add remaining ingredients. If necessary, add more water. Let stand 5 minutes. Serve as main dish with a green salad, or as a side dish. **10 servings**

Calories; 191
Protein: 6 g
Fat: 6.3 g = 29% of total calories
Potassium: 190 mg

Calcium: 30 mg
Sodium: 13 mg
Fiber: 3 g

STUFFED BIBLE BREAD POCKETS

This is ideal for a picnic. You can stuff the pockets with tuna salad, chicken salad or with split pea paste, tomato and lettuce. Assemble up to one hour before serving.

2 medium Bible Breads or whole wheat pita bread
½ cup Sans Souci Mayo
2 romaine lettuce leaves, cut in halves
1 tomato, sliced
4 slices fatfree cheese
1 cup alfalfa sprouts

Cut Bible Bread in half. Open pockets slightly and toast. Spread Sans Souci Mayo on the lower half, add lettuce, tomato, cheese and sprouts. Serve with raw veggies on the side.

4 servings

Calories per serving: 63
Protein: 2.7 g

Fat: 0.46 g = 7% of total calories
Potassium: 113 mg

CARROT - APPLE MINT

4 carrots, sliced
4 Tbsp water
1 tsp grated lemon rind
2 Granny Smith apples, cored and sliced
1 tsp mint leaves

In medium covered pan, cook carrots with water and lemon rind for 3 minutes. Add apples; continue cooking 5 minutes. Garnish with mint. Serve as side dish to turkey or chicken.

4 servings

Calories per serving: 72
Fat: 0.39 g = 5% of total calories
Potassium: 314 mg

Calcium: 25 mg
Sodium: 26 mg
Fiber: 4 g

CARROT PATE

A wonderful way to load up on beta carotene. It freezes well. With a baked potato and a salad it makes a delightful meal for me. The rest of my family enjoys it as a side dish with chicken or fish.

1 lb carrots, grated
1 cup mushrooms, sliced
1 medium onion, minced
Vegetable seasoning mix, butter-flavor granules, nutmeg, thyme, pepper to taste
½ cup vegetable stock
3 egg whites, beaten until stiff
8 oz frozen spinach, thawed and finely chopped
¼ cup feta cheese, crumbled

Cook carrots, mushrooms, onions and seasonings in stock for 10 minutes. Remove from heat. Add egg whites. Mix well. Spray a 9-inch square baking pan with cooking spray. Spread half the carrot mixture in pan. Season spinach with nutmeg and butter-flavor granules, spread spinach over carrots then cover with remaining carrots. Sprinkle cheese on top. Cover with foil. Bake at 400° for 45 minutes.

5 servings

Calories per serving: 119
Protein: 6.7 g
Fat: 4.1 g = 31% of total calories

Cholesterol: 15 mg
Fiber: 5 g

VEGETARIAN PIZZA

This pizza deserves to be called nutritious and delicious. To make the crust takes some time, therefore I usually make a double recipe and freeze one-half for later use. Squeeze as much moisture out of the zucchini as possible for a crispier crust.

6 cups zucchini, shredded
3 egg whites, slightly beaten
1 cup whole wheat flour
½ cup grated fatfree mozzarella cheese
½ cup chopped Jalapeno tofu cheese
1 large onion, chopped
1 tsp pesto
Vegetable seasoning mix and butter-flavor granules to taste

Place zucchini in cheese cloth. Squeeze to remove all liquid. Save liquid for soups. Combine zucchini with remaining ingredients. Spray two 14 x 12-inch baking pan with cooking spray. Press mixture on bottom and sides of pans. Bake crusts at 350° for 30 minutes or until crisp. Set aside.

Topping

2 cups mushrooms, sliced
1 green bell pepper, chopped
1 red onion, sliced
½ cup black olives, sliced
Italian seasoning, herb seasoning mix, vegetable seasoning
    mix, butter-flavor granules to taste
1 can (8 oz) no salt tomato paste
½ cup fatfree shredded mozzarella
½ cup crumbled feta cheese
½ cup Jalapeno tofu cheese cut in small chunks

In large bowl, combine first 5 ingredients; set aside. Spread tomato paste on the pre-baked crust. Add layer of vegetable mixture. Combine cheeses and sprinkle over top. Bake in preheated oven at 350° for 25 minutes.   **8 servings**

Calories per serving: 221
Protein: 21.5 g   Calcium: 208 mg
Fat: 8.2 g = 33% of total calories   Fiber: 3.3 g

WHOLE WHEAT LASAGNA

This is an all time favorite with guests at Sans Souci. We serve it with a salad and bran buns toasted with garlic paste. You can add 2 cups lowfat cottage cheese to the filling for additional cheese flavor. At home I make a double recipe and freeze half. It tastes even better after it is reheated.

1 zucchini, sliced
6 oz mushrooms, sliced
2 cups grated carrots
1 cup broccoli florets
1 large onion, chopped
2 cloves garlic, minced
1 yellow bell pepper, diced
½ lb spinach or nettles, chopped
Italian seasoning, vegetable seasoning mix, butter-flavor
     granules, herb seasoning mix to taste
¼ cup low sodium soy sauce or Bragg Liquid Aminos
1 cup part-skim ricotta cheese
4 oz feta cheese soaked in water to remove salt
4 oz Jalapeno tofu cheese, cut in ¼ inch pieces
9 whole wheat lasagna noodles, cooked
3 cups tomato sauce
1 cup shredded fatfree mozzarella cheese

Mix vegetables with seasonings. Saute in soy sauce for 5 minutes stirring well. In medium bowl, combine riccota, feta and Jalapeno cheese. In 13 x 9-inch baking dish, layer 3 noodles on bottom, spread ½ of vegetable mixture on noodles, then half of cheese mixture and one cup of tomato sauce. Repeat, starting with noodles. End with a layer of noodles topped with remaining tomato sauce. Top with mozzarella. Bake at 375° for 20 minutes or until lightly browned. Let stand 10 minutes before serving. **10 servings**

Calories per serving: 218   Cholesterol: 13 mg
Fat: 5.4 g = 22% of total calories   Fiber: 6 g

GLAZED SWEET POTATOES

I use sweet potatoes almost daily in soups, casseroles or just plain baked. They are high in vitamin A, fiber and carbohydrates. No sugar and butter is needed for this "better than the original" recipe. The cut surfaces of the sweet potato caramelize during baking into a delightful sweetness.

2 lb sweet potatoes, washed and cut into 2-inch cubes
1 onion, sliced
Cooking spray
Vegetable seasoning mix, butter-flavor granules,
    tarragon to taste

In large bowl, combine potatoes and onions. Spray lightly with cooking spray. Toss with seasonings. Arrange in medium baking pan. Cover and microwave for 8 minutes. Bake uncovered at 400° for 10 more minutes or until tender.   **6 servings**

Calories per serving: 168   Calcium: 48 mg
Fat: 0.35 g = 2% of total calories   Fiber: 5 g

PESTO PASTA

I met Lorel Nazzaro at the Dolphin Research Center in Florida. She grows basil and has written a book entitled *Pesto Manifesto.* Lorel inspired me to try pesto, a sauce made from basil, garlic, Parmesan cheese, pine nuts and olive oil. I tried it and liked it. You can buy pesto in any health food store.

8 asparagus spears, cut in 2-inch pieces
1 red bell pepper, cubed
1 cup sliced mushrooms
6 oz pesto, warmed at room temperature
1 lb whole wheat pasta, cooked
¼ cup non-fat grated cheese

Steam vegetables for 5 minutes. In large bowl, combine vegetables, pesto and pasta. Top with cheese. **4 servings**

Calories per serving: 573
Protein: 17.5 g
Fat: 15.7 g = 25% of total calories

Cholesterol: 12 mg
Potassium: 225 mg
Fiber: 2 g

RICE NUT LOAF WITH LEEK SAUCE

Our chef Patty and I had lunch in Yellow Springs and enjoyed the nut loaf they offered. Back at the spa we concocted this recipe from our taste memory and enjoyed our creation even more than the original loaf.

1 cup cooked brown rice
½ cup cooked split peas
½ cup frozen peas
1 small onion, minced
⅓ cup black walnuts, crushed
3 egg whites
1 Tbsp butter-flavor granules
Vegetable seasoning mix, Quick-Sip, herb seasoning mix, parsley, pepper to taste
¼ cup pecan meal

In medium bowl, mix all ingredients except pecan meal. Spray a small loaf pan with cooking spray. Dust with meal. Press mixture in pan. Bake at 350° for 40 minutes.

Sauce

2 large leeks, chopped
½ cup white wine
2 Tbsp lemon juice

In saucepan, cook all ingredients for 8 minutes. Puree in blender and serve over loaf.   **6 servings**

Calories per serving: 205   Calcium: 52 mg
Fat: 6.5 g = 28% of total calories   Sodium: 40 mg
Potassium: 334 mg   Fiber: 3 g

FITNESS SWIRLS

6 whole wheat lasagna noodles

Sauce

2 cups no salt tomato sauce
1 large tomato, chopped
1 large carrot, finely shredded
½ cup chopped onions
2 cloves garlic, minced
½ tsp basil
½ tsp oregano
½ tsp fennel seed

Filling

3 cups fatfree riccota or Fitness Cheese
¼ cup Sans Souci Mayo
2 Tbsp chopped fresh parsley
¼ tsp nutmeg
½ lb fresh asparagus cut into 3-inch pieces
1 cup fatfree grated cheese

Cook the noodles al dente. Drain and rinse with cold water. Set aside. In medium saucepan, combine sauce ingredients. Cook for 10 minutes. Set aside. In medium bowl combine filling ingredients except asparagus and cheese. Coat each noodle with 3 Tbsp of the filling along its entire length. Top with asparagus. Roll up and place in small casserole. Pour sauce over noodles. Sprinkle cheese on top. Bake at 350° for 30 minutes. **6 servings**

Calories per serving: 223   Calcium: 507 mg
Fat: 1.4 g = 5% of total calories   Fiber: 3 g

BULGUR STIR FRY

1 cup bulgur wheat
2 cups boiling water
1 medium onion, chopped
1 red bell pepper, chopped
1 zucchini, sliced
1 cup broccoli florets
1 cup cauliflower florets
1 cup pea pods
1 clove garlic, minced
2 Tbsp Quick-Sip or low sodium soy sauce
Dill, marjoram, basil, parsley, vegetable seasoning mix, herb
    seasoning mix to taste
2 Tbsp lemon juice
3 oz feta cheese
3 oz fatfree Cheddar cheese

In large bowl, cover bulgur with boiling water. Let stand 1 hour. Drain. Simmer vegetables and garlic in Quick-Sip for 5 minutes. Add seasonings and lemon juice. Mix all ingredients, except Cheddar cheese. Place in medium baking pan. Top with Cheddar cheese. Broil until cheese is melted. Garnish with tomato slices. **6 servings**

Calories per serving: 218
Fat: 6.7 g = 28% of total calories
Cholesterol: 25 mg

Potassium: 422 mg
Calcium: 182 mg
Fiber: 3 g

PASTA PRIMAVERA

8 oz whole wheat spiral noodles or oat bran noodles
1 cup broccoli florets
1 cup cauliflower florets
1 cup asparagus, cut in 2-inch pieces
1 cup snow peas
1 cup sliced mushrooms
1 cup fresh or frozen corn
1 small zucchini, cut in chunks
1 red bell pepper, chopped
¼ cup fatfree Ranch dressing
¼ cup finely minced parsley
3 oz Jalapeno tofu cheese, chopped
3 garlic cloves, minced
Vegetable seasoning mix, herb seasoning mix, butter-flavor
    granules to taste

    Cook the noodles al dente. Drain and rinse with cold water. Set aside. Steam all vegetables for 5′ minutes. Add dressing, parsley, cheese and seasonings. Mix well. Place cooked noodles in bowl. Spread vegetables on top and toss gently. Serve on lettuce leaf. Garnish with tomato slices. **7 servings**

Calories per serving: 183   Cholesterol: 2 mg
Fat: 1.9 g = 9% of total calories   Fiber: 4 g

TABBOULI

1 cup bulgur wheat
2 cups hot water
4 scallions, chopped
1 large tomato, diced
1 red bell pepper, diced
½ cup cauliflower florets
½ cup chopped fresh parsley

¼ cup fatfree Ranch dressing
¼ cup lemon juice
2 Tbsp chopped mint
2 Tbsp radish sprouts
Herb seasoning mix,
    oregano, coriander to taste

Soak bulgur in hot water 1 hour. Drain. Add remaining ingredients and mix well. Refrigerate 1 hour before serving.

6 servings

Calories per serving: 227
Fat: 2.1 g = 8% of total calories
Cholesterol: 0.67 mg
Potassium: 910 gm

Sodium: 64 gm
Calcium: 99 mg
Fiber: 3 g

STUFFED ZUCCHINI

4 medium zucchini
2 egg whites, slightly beaten
1 cup cooked wild rice, brown rice or couscous
1 tomato, chopped
1 stalk celery, chopped
½ cup feta cheese
Vegetable seasoning mix, butter-flavor granules, pepper, garlic powder, onion powder, dill weed to taste

Halve zucchini lengthwise, scoop out most of the pulp leaving a 1/2-inch thick shell. Set aside. Chop pulp and mix with remaining ingredients. Fill shells with mixture. Place filled shells in baking dish, cover. Bake at 350° for 40 minutes.

4 servings

Calories per serving: 261
Protein: 14 g
Fat: 6.8 g = 23% of total calories

Potassium: 730 mg
Calcium: 184 mg

SPAGHETTI SQUASH WITH SAUCE

With fork poke holes in a medium spaghetti squash. Bake at 350° for 50 minutes or cook in microwave on high for 20 minutes or until soft to touch. Cut in half, remove seeds. Scrape squash with fork. It is stringy, resembling spaghetti. Place in bowl, set aside.

Sauce

8 oz low sodium tomato sauce
2 fresh tomatoes, chopped
1 green bell pepper, chopped
3 scallions, chopped
6 mushrooms, chopped
1 celery stalk, chopped
2 garlic cloves, crushed
Italian seasoning, fines herbes, herb pepper, vegetable
    seasoning mix, butter-flavor granules, herb seasoning mix
    to taste
3 oz fatfree grated cheese

Mix all ingredients except cheese.   Simmer for 6 minutes. Divide squash in 6 serving dishes. To each serving add equal portions of sauce. Top with cheese. You can top with cooked, chopped chicken or turkey breast for more protein. **6 servings**

Calories per serving: 59   Calcium: 30 mg
Fat: 0.88 g = 13% of total calories   Sodium: 12 mg
Potassium: 621 mg   Fiber: 4 g

CABBAGE ROLLS WITH WALNUT STUFFING

1 small onion, chopped
1 clove garlic, minced
1 small celery stalk, chopped
½ cup red bell pepper, chopped
½ lb spinach, chopped
1 small zucchini, grated
2 Tbsp Jensen's Broth
2 Tbsp Quick-Sip
2 Tbsp low sodium soy sauce
1 cup cooked brown rice
1 cup walnuts, chopped
1 cup split pea paste or frozen peas
3 egg whites, slightly beaten
Vegetable seasoning mix, bay leaf powder, herb seasoning
    mix and butter-flavor granules to taste
1 Chinese cabbage head, blanched to soften leaves
1 cup sauerkraut
¼ cup apple juice
¼ cup lemon juice
2 tomatoes, sliced

In skillet, simmer vegetables with broth, Quick-Sip and soy sauce for 5 minutes. Remove from heat. Mix with rice, walnuts, pea paste, egg whites and seasonings. Place 2 to 3 tablespoons of the mixture in each cabbage leaf. Roll up each leaf lengthwise, fold in the ends of cabbage leaf. Place cabbage rolls in a 9-inch square baking pan. Chop up remaining cabbage, mix with sauerkraut. Place on top of cabbage rolls. Mix apple and lemon juice, pour over cabbage rolls. Top with tomato slices. Cover and bake at 350° for 40 minutes. Garnish each serving with 1 tsp fatfree yogurt.   **10 servings**

Calories per serving: 161
Fat: 7 g = 39% of total calories   Calcium: 110 gm
Potassium: 662 gm   Fiber: 5 g

SOY BEAN PATTIES

⅔ cup edible soy beans
3 cups water
1⅓ cups rolled oats
1 onion, minced
1 Tbsp Quick-Sip
1 tsp each oregano, basil, minced garlic, butter-flavor granules
      and vegetable seasoning mix
2 egg whites, slightly beaten
2 Tbsp whole wheat bread crumbs

Wash, then soak beans in water overnight. Discard soaking water. Add 3 cups fresh water and boil 40 minutes or until tender. In electric blender, puree soy beans with 1¼ cups cooking liquid. In mixing bowl, combine all ingredients except bread crumbs. Mix well. Form into patties. Dust with bread crumbs. Cook in nonstick skillet over medium heat on each side until golden brown. Serve with tomato sauce or nettle souffle.

4 servings

Calories per serving: 146
Fat: 2.6 g = 16% of total calories   Calcium: 58 mg
Potassium: 259 mg   Fiber: 3 g

SPINACH or NETTLE SOUFFLE

1½ cups water
2 Tbsp arrowroot flour
½ cup nonfat dry milk, dry form
4 oz. feta cheese, crumbled
Vegetable seasoning mix, herb seasoning mix, butter-flavor
    granules to taste
1 lb spinach or nettles, steamed and chopped

In medium pan, combine water and flour until smooth. Bring to a boil, stirring well. Add dry milk, cheese and seasonings, stirring continuously. Add spinach and bring to a boil while stirring. Serve with soy bean patties or as a side dish to any dinner. **4 servings**

Calories per serving: 146
Protein: 10 g
Fat: 6.4 g = 38% of total calories
Cholesterol: 27 mg

Potassium: 692 mg
Calcium: 400 mg
Fiber: 3 g

SANS SOUCI GOES MEXICAN

2 Bible Breads or whole wheat pita bread
2 cups split pea paste
1 head Bibb lettuce, chopped
1 tomato, chopped
3 scallions, chopped
1 cup tomato sauce
½ cup shredded fatfree cheese
Herb seasoning mix and chili powder to taste

Cut Bible Bread edges, open the two rounds and toast. Spread pea paste evenly on bread halves. Top with lettuce, tomato, scallions, tomato sauce and cheese, in that order. Season with herb seasoning mix. **4 servings**

Calories per serving: 200
Fat: 5 g = 23% of total calorie

Cholesterol: 14 mg
Fiber: 5 g

SEED BALLS

3 egg whites
1 cup seed sauce or split pea paste
1 red bell pepper, minced
1 zucchini, minced
2 celery stalks, minced
3 scallions, minced
3 Tbsp whole wheat bread crumbs
1 Tbsp parsley flakes
Dill, basil, caraway seed, vegetable seasoning mix, herb
    seasoning mix to taste

In medium bowl, lightly beat egg whites with fork. Add remaining ingredients. Form into 1-inch balls. Makes about 12 balls. Bake at 375° for 30 minutes. Serve with spinach souffle and baked potato. **4 servings**

Calories per serving: 34
Fat: .41 g = 11% of total calories   Calcium: 42 mg
Potassium: 279 mg   Fiber: 2 g

BAKED STUFFED POTATOES

3 large potatoes
1 cup Fitness Cheese or lowfat cottage cheese
¼ cup Jalapeno tofu cheese, chopped
⅓ cup chopped onion
Dill, parsley, garlic powder, caraway seed, butter-flavor
    granules to taste
2 egg whites, stiffly beaten
½ tsp paprika

Bake potatoes until almost done. Cut in half lengthwise and scoop out most of the inside with a spoon. Save the skins for stuffing. Mash scooped out potato and mix fitness and tofu cheese, onion and seasonings. Fold in egg whites. Stuff the potato skins with the mashed potato mixture. Place in non-stick baking pan. Sprinkle with paprika. Bake at 400° for 10 minutes until hot and golden brown. Serve with a salad, as a main course or as a side dish. **6 servings**

Calories per serving: 123
Fat: 0.66 g = 5% of total calories
Cholesterol: 3 mg

Potassium: 548 mg
Calcium: 179 mg
Fiber: 3 g

POTATO - ONION CASSEROLE

6 medium red potatoes, unpeeled
1 large onion, sliced
½ cup feta cheese, crumbled
Herb seasoning mix, vegetable seasoning mix, paprika, butter-
    flavored granules to taste

   Slice potatoes and layer in medium baking dish to cover
bottom. Add half of the onion slices, sprinkle half of the feta
cheese and seasonings. Repeat with remaining potatoes,
onion rings, feta cheese and seasonings. Cover and bake at
350° for 40 minutes or until done. Serve as a side dish or as a
main meal with a large salad.   **6 servings**

Calories per serving: 163
Fat: 4.2 g = 23% of total calories   Calcium: 107 mg
Potassium: 490 mg   Fiber: 4 g

BAKED POLENTA CASSEROLE

3½ cups water   ½ cup feta cheese
1 cup whole grain yellow cornmeal   4 egg whites
1 tsp butter-flavor granules   ½ tsp paprika
1 cup Fitness Cheese

   In medium saucepan, bring water to a boil. In a slow,
steady stream add cornmeal to boiling water, stirring constantly with wire whisk or wooden spoon. Add butter-flavor
granules. Cook 5 minutes stirring often. In medium baking
dish, spread half of polenta. Layer half of the feta and Fitness
Cheese. Layer with remaining polenta, egg whites and
cheeses. Sprinkle paprika on top. Bake at 400° for 20 minutes.
                                        6 servings

Calories per serving: 178   Potassium: 450 mg
Fat: 4.9 g = 25% of total calories   Calcium: 250 mg
Cholesterol: 18 mg   Fiber: 4 g

PATTY'S EGGPLANT QUICHE

4½ cups cubed, unpeeled eggplant
¼ cup water
1 Tbsp butter-flavor granules
1 medium onion, chopped
2 cloves garlic, minced
½ tsp each, herb seasoning mix, oregano, basil and vegetable
    seasoning mix
Dash cayenne
10 asparagus spears cut into 2-inch pieces
⅔ cup soy milk
3 egg whites, slightly beaten
2 cups part-skim mozzarella cheese

In large skillet, add eggplant, water, butter-flavor granules, onions and garlic. Simmer for 2 minutes. Cover and continue cooking 5 minutes, stirring a few times. Add spices and mix well. Line bottom of 10-inch pie pan with asparagus spears. Spoon eggplant mixture over them. Combine milk, egg whites and cheese; pour over vegetables. Bake at 375° for 30 minutes. **6 servings**

Calories per serving: 72   Calcium: 66 mg
Fat: 1.9 g = 23% of total calories   Fiber: 2.8 g

POLENTA WITH TOMATO SAUCE

1 onion, minced
1 zucchini, chopped
½ cup celery, coarsely chopped
1 ripe tomato, chopped
1 cup no salt tomato sauce
Basil, parsley, pepper, vegetable seasoning mix and butter-
    flavored granules to taste
3½ cups water
1 cup whole grain yellow cornmeal
½ cup fatfree shredded mozzarella cheese
½ cup crumbled feta cheese

In large skillet, simmer onion, zucchini and celery in 2 Tbsp water until tender. Add tomato, tomato sauce and seasonings. Bring to a boil. Cover and reduce heat. Simmer about 10 minutes. Set aside. In medium saucepan, bring water to a boil. In a slow, steady stream, add cornmeal to boiling water. Stir constantly with wooden spoon. Lower heat. Cook 10 minutes, stirring often to keep from sticking. Spoon polenta onto medium baking dish. Top with sauce. Sprinkle cheeses on top. Bake at 350° for 10 minutes or until golden brown.

4 servings

Calories per serving: 168
Fat: 1.9 g = 10% of total calories
Cholesterol: 2 mg

Potassium: 594 mg
Calcium: 130 mg
Fiber: 8 g

CHAPTER 14
SEAFOOD ENTREES

FISH IN A POUCH

1 lb white fish, cut into 5 pieces
1 red bell pepper, julienned
1 cup green beans, halved lengthwise
1 carrot, julienned
1 onion, cut into rings
¼ cup of lemon juice
1 tsp thyme
Herb seasoning mix, vegetable seasoning mix, butter-flavor
    granules and pepper to taste

Set each fish piece in the center of a 12-inch square of aluminum foil. Arrange ⅕ of each vegetable on each fillet. Combine lemon juice and seasonings. Pour over each fish mixture. Fold foil into tight packets. Bake at 450° for 15 minutes or until fish flakes easily with a fork. **5 servings**

Calories per serving: 161
Fat: 5.5 g = 31% of total calories   Sodium: 54 mg
Cholesterol: 55 mg   Calcium: 32 mg
Potassium: 522 mg   Fiber: 2 g

FETTUCCINE WITH SALMON

1½ cups sliced mushrooms
1 small yellow squash or zucchini, sliced
1 tomato, diced
2 Tbsp chopped onions
¼ cup red wine
1 Tbsp whole wheat flour
½ cup skim milk
Basil, pepper, oregano and butter-flavor granules to taste
1 cup drained and flaked salmon or tuna
½ cup frozen peas, thawed
1 Tbsp fresh minced parsley
8 oz whole wheat fettuccine, cooked and drained
6 lemon wedges

In medium skillet, simmer mushrooms, squash, tomato and onion in wine for 10 minutes. Mix flour and milk until smooth. Add to vegetables with seasonings. Cook 2 minutes, stir in salmon, peas and parsley. Heat and serve over fettuccine. Garnish with lemon.   **4 servings**

Calories per serving: 288
Fat: 2.6 g = 8% of total calories   Calcium: 93 mg
Cholesterol: 11 mg   Sodium: 1098 mg
Potassium: 567 mg   Fiber: 4 g

FISH ALMONDINE

1 lb white fish, cut in 5 equal pieces
Vegetable seasoning mix and butter-flavor granules to taste
2 lemons, thinly sliced
2 Tbsp Fitness Cheese
1 tsp dill weed
1 Tbsp lemon juice
2 Tbsp almond slivers, toasted

In medium baking dish, place single layer of fish. Season both sides with vegetable seasoning mix and butter-flavor granules. Top with lemon slices. Cover and microwave for 10 minutes or until fish flakes easily with a fork. While fish is cooking, mix cheese, dill and lemon juice. Place fish on serving plate. Top with sauce and sprinkle with almonds. Serve with baked stuffed potato. **5 servings**

Calories per serving: 136
Protein: 18 g
Fat: 6.2 g = 41% of total calories
Cholesterol: 55 mg

Potassium: 323 mg
Calcium: 15 mg
Sodium: 48 mg
Fiber: 0.26 g

BAKED FISH

1 lb white fish
1 tsp tarragon
Vegetable seasoning mix and butter-flavor granules to taste
2 egg whites
Juice of ½ lemon
½ cup oat bran
½ cup whole wheat bread crumbs

Cut fish in 5 equal pieces. Sprinkle with seasonings. In small bowl, lightly beat egg whites, mix in lemon juice. In medium bowl, combine bran and bread crumbs. Dip fillets in egg mixture then into bran mixture. Coat fish on both sides, pressing coating with your hands. Spray baking pan with cooking spray. Place fish on a baking pan. Bake at 500° for 8 minutes or until fish is done. Garnish with lemon.   **5 servings**

Calories per serving: 154
Protein: 20 g
Fat: 5.6 g = 33% of total calories
Cholesterol: 55 mg

Potassium: 376 mg
Calcium: 11 mg
Sodium: 70 mg
Fiber: 2 g

SALMON MOUSSE

1 envelope unflavored gelatin
¼ cup water
1 can (16 oz) salmon, skin removed and well drained
1 cup Fitness Cheese or part skim riccota cheese
2 Tbsp fatfree cucumber dressing
1 Tbsp lemon juice
1 Tbsp grated onion
1 Tbsp minced dill
1 Tbsp minced parsley
White pepper and butter-flavor granules to taste

In small saucepan, dissolve gelatin in boiling water. In electric blender, puree salmon, cheese, dressing and lemon juice. In medium mixing bowl, combine all ingredients, mixing well. Place in refrigerator for 10 minutes to allow mousse to partially set. Spray a medium fish mold with cooking spray. Pour in mixture. Chill 3 hours. Unmold the mousse on a platter and serve.   **6 servings**

Calories per serving: 138
Protein: 18 g
Fat: 5 g = 33% of total calories
Cholesterol: 43 mg

Potassium: 399 mg
Calcium: 249 mg
Sodium: 259 mg

SEAFOOD DIVAN

8 oz broccoli
8 oz cauliflower
Vegetable seasoning mix and butter-flavor granules to taste
6 oz crab meat or white fish, cut into bite-size pieces
6 oz shrimp, cleaned
Juice of 1 lemon

Cut broccoli and cauliflower in bite-size pieces. Season with vegetable seasoning mix and butter-flavor granules. Arrange in medium baking dish. Spoon seafood over broccoli. Sprinkle with lemon juice.

Sauce

1½ cup skim milk or soy milk
2 Tbsp arrowroot flour
4 oz feta cheese, crumbled
½ tsp paprika

In small mixing bowl, stir together ¼ cup milk with flour until smooth. In medium saucepan, bring 1 cup of milk to a boil. Add flour mixture to milk, stirring constantly. Cook over medium heat 1 minute or until thick and bubbly. Reduce heat. Add cheese and stir to melt. Pour sauce over seafood to cover. Sprinkle with paprika. Bake at 375° for 30 minutes or until fish is done.   **6 servings**

Calories per serving: 130
Protein: 13 g
Fat: 4.9 g = 34% of total calories
Cholesterol: 65

Potassium: 383 mg
Calcium: 385 mg
Sodium: 369 mg
Fiber: 3 g

SHRIMP CREPES WITH LEMON SAUCE

8 Crepes, see Crepe Suzette recipe

Filling

5 scallions, chopped
1 red bell pepper, chopped
1 Tbsp wine or water
1 Tbsp lemon juice
1 clove garlic, minced
1 lb peeled, cooked shrimp, cut in half
Dash of red bell pepper sauce, butter-flavor granules, vegetable seasoning mix, dill to taste

In medium saucepan, cook scallions, pepper, wine, lemon juice and garlic for 5 minutes. Stir in remaining ingredients. Place 2 Tbsp of shrimp filling in the center and roll up each crepe. Place crepes in a baking dish side by side. Heat at 350° for about 10 minutes.

Sauce

¼ cup white wine
3 Tbsp lemon juice
1 leek, chopped

In saucepan, cook all ingredients for 10 minutes. Puree in blender and serve over crepes. **8 servings**

Calories per serving: 157
Protein: 16 g
Fat: 1.5 g = 9% of total calories
Cholesterol: 100 mg

Potassium: 327 mg
Calcium: 103 mg
Sodium: 121 mg
Fiber: 3 g

TUNA BURGER

1 can (8 oz) water-packed
    tuna, no salt added
1 slice whole wheat bread
2 oz skim milk
2 scallions, chopped

2 egg whites
1 small stalk celery, chopped
1 tsp grated lemon peel
1 tsp lemon juice
½ tsp rosemary

Herb seasoning mix, vegetable seasoning mix, butter-flavor granules to taste

Drain tuna. Soak bread in milk then squeeze dry and crumble. Discard rest of milk. Mix all ingredients and form into 5 burgers. In nonstick skillet, cook on both sides until brown. Serve with toasted bran buns, Sans Souci Mayo, lettuce, tomato slice and onion slice. **5 servings**

Calories per serving: 118
Fat: 4 g = 31% of total calories
Cholesterol: 16 mg
Potassium: 441

Calcium: 143
Sodium: 84
Fiber: 5 g

VEGETABLE SEAFOOD KEBABS

8 jumbo shrimp, cleaned
4 mushrooms, halved
1 green bell pepper,
    cut in 1-inch squares

1 summer squash,
    cut in ½-inch slices
8 cherry tomatoes
1 onion, cut in chunks

Vegetable seasoning mix, butter-flavor granules, herb seasoning mix to taste

Soak skewers in water to prevent burning. Thread ingredients alternately on 2 skewers. Sprinkle with seasonings. Broil 6 to 8 minutes, turning occasionally. **2 servings**

Calories per serving: 90
Protein: 8 g
Fat: 0.98 g = 10% of total calories
Cholesterol: 43 mg

Potassium: 452 mg
Calcium: 44 mg
Sodium: 51 mg
Fiber: 4 g

CHAPTER 15
POULTRY

PATTY'S ORANGE TURKEY

½ cup orange juice
2 tsp arrowroot flour
3 Tbsp cold water
1 Tbsp lemon juice
1 green bell pepper, cut into slices
1 onion, sliced
1 orange, peeled and sliced
Chili powder, vegetable seasoning mix, parsley to taste
12 oz cooked turkey breast, cut in thin strips

In medium saucepan, bring orange juice to a boil. In small bowl, dissolve flour in water. Add to boiling juice, stir until it starts bubbling. Add remaining ingredients except turkey. Boil for 6 minutes. Add turkey to heat. To serve, place turkey in center, surrounded by orange slices and pepper. **4 servings**

Calories per serving: 200
Fat: 0.97 g = 4% of total calories   Calcium: 48 mg
Cholesterol: 71 mg   Sodium: 56 mg
Potassium: 600 mg   Fiber: 3 g

THANKSGIVING - or ANY DAY TURKEY

6 slices no salt cooked turkey breast

Stuffing

¾ cup cooked brown rice
2 Tbsp whole wheat bread crumbs
1 cup steamed and diced mixed vegetables
½ cup Fitness Cheese
¼ cup feta cheese, crumbled
1 Tbsp chopped fresh parsley
1 Tbsp onion flakes
Vegetable seasoning mix, herb seasoning mix, butter-flavor
    granules to taste

    Mix all ingredients. Place ⅙ of the stuffing on each turkey slice, roll up and secure with toothpicks.

Sauce

¼ cup white wine
3 Tbsp lemon juice
1 leek chopped
Vegetable seasoning mix and butter-flavor granules to taste

    In small saucepan, combine all ingredients. Cook over medium heat for 8 minutes. Puree in blender. Pour over turkey rolls. Serve with steamed brussels sprouts, baked sweet potato and Raw Cranberry Delight, see recipe.

6 servings

Calories per serving: 198
Fat: 3 g = 14% of total calories   Calcium: 160 mg
Cholesterol: 56 mg   Sodium: 189 mg
Potassium: 433 mg   Fiber: 2 g

PEA POD ALMOND CHICKEN

½ cup water
3 Tbsp low sodium soy sauce or Quick-Sip
4 garlic cloves, minced
Vegetable seasoning mix, herb seasoning mix, butter-flavor
    granules, Jensen's Broth to taste
1 lb chicken breast, skinned, boned and cut into 2-inch pieces
1 lb pea pods
2 Tbsp toasted almond slivers

   In medium casserole dish, mix water, soy sauce, garlic and seasonings. Add chicken and marinate 10 minutes. Cover and bake at 350° for 40 minutes. Add pea pods, mix with chicken and sauce. Bake for an additional 3 minutes. Add almonds. Serve with couscous or rice.   **5 servings**

Calories per serving: 161
Fat: 5.5 g = 31% of total calories   Calcium: 60 mg
Cholesterol: 42 mg   Sodium: 401 mg
Potassium: 352 mg   Fiber: 3 g

HAWAIIAN CHICKEN

1 lb skinless chicken breast, cut in 2-inch pieces
Ginger, vegetable seasoning mix, herb seasoning mix, butter-
    flavored granules to taste
1 green bell pepper, cut in rings
1 medium onion, sliced
½ pineapple, cubed
1 orange, sliced
½ cup orange juice

   Sprinkle chicken with seasonings. In medium baking dish, layer chicken, pepper, onion, pineapple and orange. Pour orange juice on top. Cover and bake at 375° for 45 minutes. Serve with rice or couscous.   **6 servings**

Calories per serving: 225
Fat: 4.1 g = 16% of total calories   Cholesterol: 69 mg
Potassium: 470 mg   Calcium: 37 mg

PAELLA

½ lb skinless chicken breast, cut in 1-inch pieces
½ lb scallops or shrimp
1 medium onion, chopped
½ cup Jensen's Broth
3 Tbsp Quick-Sip or low sodium soy sauce
3 cloves garlic, minced
Saffron, basil, oregano, paprika, pepper, vegetable seasoning
    mix, butter-flavor granules to taste
1 cup chopped tomatoes
1 cup chopped red bell pepper
1 cup sliced mushrooms
1 cup chopped celery
3 Tbsp chopped fresh parsley
3 cups cooked brown rice

In large skillet, combine first 6 ingredients. Simmer for 20 minutes. Add seasonings, tomatoes, red bell pepper, mushrooms and celery. Simmer for an additional 8 minutes. Add parsley and serve over bed of rice.   **6 servings**

Calories per serving: 252
Fat: 3.6 g = 13% of total calories   Potassium: 479 mg
Cholesterol: 93 mg   Calcium: 57 mg

CHICKEN PAPRIKASH

1 lb skinless chicken breast, cut into fillets
1 tsp each paprika, butter-flavor granules and vegetable
    seasoning mix
1 cup skim buttermilk
2 cups sliced mushrooms
½ cup chopped onion
½ cup chopped green bell pepper
½ cup chopped celery
¼ cup dry wine
1 cup condensed skim milk
3 cups cooked whole wheat noodles

    Season chicken with seasonings. In flat baking dish place chicken in single layer. Cover with buttermilk. Marinate for 2 hours. Bake at 400° for 25 minutes. In medium skillet, simmer vegetables in wine for 8 minutes. Add milk. Combine with chicken. Serve over bed of noodles. Garnish with parsley.

6 servings

Calories per serving: 307
Fat: 4.4 g = 13% of total calories   Potassium: 622 mg
Cholesterol: 71 mg   Calcium: 201 mg

PATTY'S POT PIE

2½ cups skim milk
¼ cup arrowroot flour
3 oz feta cheese, crumbled
1 lb chicken breast, cut in 1-inch squares
2 cups cubed potatoes
1 cup sliced carrots
1 cup cubed red bell pepper
1 cup sliced mushrooms
¾ cup chopped scallions
3 Tbsp low sodium soy sauce or Quick-Sip
Herb seasoning mix, vegetable seasoning mix, butter-flavor
    granules, tarragon powder to taste
1 cup corn
1 cup frozen or fresh peas
4 oz fatfree Cheddar cheese, shredded

In small bowl, combine ½ cup milk with flour until smooth. In medium pan, bring remaining milk to a boil. Add flour mixture stirring constantly until bubbly and smooth. Mix in feta cheese to melt. Set aside. In large skillet, simmer next 8 ingredients for 10 minutes. Add corn, peas and sauce, mix well. Divide mixture into 6 oven-proof soup bowls, top with Cheddar cheese. Bake at 375° for 30 minutes.   **6 servings**

Calories per serving: 320
Fat: 6.5 g = 18% of total calories   Calcium: 229 mg
Potassium: 846 mg   Fiber: 4.1 g

CHAPTER 16
DESSERTS

SWISS RICE FRUIT CREAM

2 Tbsp gelatin
1 cup water
2 bananas
1 cup cooked brown rice
3 Tbsp apple juice concentrate, undiluted
1 tsp vanilla
1 tsp grated lemon rind
1 cup Fitness Cheese
1 kiwi
8 strawberries

Dissolve gelatin in hot water and place in blender. Add all remaining ingredients except kiwi and strawberries. Process in blender until smooth. Place in 6 long stem dessert dishes. Chill for 1 hour. Garnish with kiwi and strawberry slices before serving. **6 servings**

Calories per serving: 134
Fat: 1.3 g = 9% of total calories
Cholesterol: 3 mg
Potassium: 434 mg
Calcium: 86 mg
Sodium: 32 mg
Fiber: 3 g

CARROT - APRICOT SOUFFLE

½ lb carrots, cut in 1-inch chunks
⅓ cup water
3 lemon slices with peel
¼ lb dried apricots
1 tsp low-calorie sweetener
4 egg whites, stiffly beaten
2 Tbsp pecan meal

In medium pan, cook carrots, water and lemon slices for 6 minutes. Add apricots and simmer until all water is absorbed. Puree in blender until smooth. Add sweetener. Pour into mixing bowl. Fold in egg whites. Spray a 2-quart baking dish with cooking spray. Dust with pecan meal. Pour mixture into baking dish. Bake in preheated oven at 350° for 40 minutes. Serve immediately.   **6 servings**

Calories per serving: 93   Sodium: 52 mg
Fat: 2.1 g = 20% of total calories   Calcium: 22 mg
Potassium: 427 mg   Fiber: 3 g

RAW CRANBERRY DELIGHT

1 package unflavored gelatin
¼ cup boiling water
1 orange
½ cup sprouted sunflower seed, optional
1 can (12 oz) frozen apple juice concentrate, undiluted
4 cups fresh or frozen cranberries

Dissolve gelatin in boiling water. Wash orange and cut, unpeeled, into sections. In food processor, blend orange, seed, apple juice and gelatin until smooth. Add cranberries and process, leaving some of the cranberries chunky. Refrigerate for 1 hour. Serve as a refreshing dessert with pear halves and mint or as a side dish with turkey dinner.   **8 servings**

Calories per serving: 126
Fat: .33 g = 2% of total calories   Calcium: 22 mg
Potassium: 330 mg   Sodium: 16 mg

BANANA - STRAWBERRY SAUCE

1 ripe banana, sliced
6 fresh large strawberries, washed and sliced
1 cup Fitness Cheese
1 tsp vanilla
1 tsp low calorie sweetener

In electric blender, blend all ingredients until smooth. Use as a refreshing dessert, as a topping on crepes or on freshly toasted whole wheat bagels. **3 servings**

Calories per serving: 92
Fat: 1.45 g = 14% of total calories   Calcium: 180 mg
Cholesterol: 5 mg   Sodium: 61 mg
Potassium: 355 mg   Fiber: 2 g

FRUITY DELIGHT

1 cup each of dried apricots, peaches and pears
1 cup almond butter
½ cup rolled oats
½ cup fatfree granola
¼ cup apple juice concentrate, undiluted
Dash of rum extract
¼ cup pecan meal

Chop dried fruit in the food processor. In large bowl, combine all ingredients except pecan meal. Mix well to bind. Form into small balls. Roll in pecan meal. Keep refrigerated. **16 servings**

Calories per serving: 140
Protein: 3.5 g   Calcium: 56 mg
Fat: 7 g = 45% of total calories   Sodium: 6 mg
Potassium: 444 mg   Fiber: 3 g

RAW APPLE DESSERT

4 medium apples, unpeeled and sliced
1 Tbsp lemon juice
10 dates
1 cup sprouted sunflower seed
½ tsp vanilla
½ tsp cinnamon

In food processor, blend all ingredients until smooth. Garnish with fresh strawberries and kiwi slices before serving.

10 servings

Calories per serving: 78
Fat: 1.6 g = 18% of total calories
Potassium: 139 mg

Calcium: 12 mg
Sodium: 3 mg
Fiber: 3 g

RHUBARB COMPOTE

3 cups rhubarb, cut in 1-inch chunks
2 cups water
½ cup honey

In medium pan, combine all ingredients. Boil for 8 minutes. Serve over cheese cake, rice pudding or eat as dessert.

8 servings

Calories per serving: 48
Fat: 0.1 g = 2% of total calories

Potassium: 137 mg
Calcium: 40 mg

SANS SOUCI ICE CREAM

This is a delightful, simple summer dessert, getting an "A+" from Sans Souci guests.

2 cups frozen banana chunks
1 cup frozen raspberries
½ tsp vanilla, optional

Slightly thaw fruit, place in food processor. Use metal blade and process until consistency of soft ice cream. Garnish with pecan meal and serve immediately.   **6 servings**

Calories per serving: 71
Fat: 1.1 g = 14% of total calories   Calcium: 9 mg
Potassium: 261 mg   Fiber: 2 g

ROTE GRUTZE, GERMAN FRUIT PUDDING

¼ cup arrowroot flour
1½ cup pineapple juice
2 cups raspberries, pureed
2 Tbsp honey
1 tsp vanilla

In saucepan, dissolve flour in pineapple juice. Bring to a boil; stirring constantly. Add remaining ingredients. Simmer until slightly thickened, stirring frequently. Cool. Pour into individual glass dishes and chill. Garnish with berries, yogurt or edible blossoms such as violets, rose petals, or marigolds.
8 servings

Calories per serving: 73   Calcium: 15 mg
Fat: 0.21 g = 3% of total calories   Sodium: 0.8 mg
Potassium: 113 mg   Fiber: 2 g

SUSIE'S TRUFFLES

When Shirley Maxwell, the food editor of this book, tried our truffles she exclaimed; "Susie, these truffles are right up there with a Mercedes Benz, the color blue and the best things in life. They taste wonderful - and to think that they are good for you". Shirley, you are not alone, everybody who trys the truffles likes them.

You can freeze the truffles for 2 months. Depending on the degree of softness of the almond butter you may have to adjust the amount of dry ingredients to achieve a firm consistency. Truffles made with almond butter have a marzipan-like taste. You can replace almond butter with peanut butter and almond extract with 2 Tbsp carob powder for a more chocolate-like taste. Use the "natural" peanut butter with no salt added and discard the oil which has accumulated on top.

Reserve truffles for special occasions. Eat no more than two at a time, as they are high in calories.

1 cup almond butter
¾ cup honey, warmed
2 tsp almond extract
1 cup rolled oats
1 cup Nutty Rice cereal
½ cup rolled barley
½ cup fatfree granola
¼ cup pecan meal or wheat germ

In large bowl, combine almond butter and honey until well mixed and smooth. Stir in almond extract. Add oats, rice, barley and granola; mix well. Form into 1-inch balls. Roll in pecan meal. **60 truffles**

Calories per serving: 62 per each truffle
Protein: 1.7 g
Fat: 2.7 g = 39% of total calories
Potassium: 63 mg
Calcium: 15 mg
Sodium: 1 mg
Fiber: 1 g

SUSIE'S TRUFFLES VARIATION

Shaping Susie's Truffles and rolling them in the pecan meal is the most time-consuming part of the process. One day I was in a hurry, so I developed this variation. Instead of rolling the truffles into the 1-inch balls, I used a baking pan to make a solid layer of the mixture, then cut into 1-inch squares. This is handy for large parties or weddings. Here's how to do it.

Pour the mixture into a large flat pan and press into a ½-inch thick layer using back of wooden spoon, finish pressing and shaping with slightly dampened palm. If desired, top with All Fruit Preserves and Nutty Rice cereal. Cut in 1-inch squares.

LOW-FAT CHEESE CAKE

8 oz Fitness Cheese or part skim ricotta cheese
3 egg whites
1 egg
3 Tbsp honey
¼ cup cornstarch or pecan meal
2 tsp grated lemon peel
1 tsp vanilla
1 tsp baking powder
2 Tbsp pecan meal
1 cup fresh raspberries or strawberries

In large bowl, combine cheese, egg whites, egg and honey. Beat with electric mixer until smooth. Add remaining ingredients, except pecan meal and fruit. Mix well. Spray a 9-inch springform pan with cooking spray. Coat with pecan meal. Pour mixture in pan. Bake in preheated 350° oven for 60 minutes. Cool and decorate with fruit or Rhubarb Compote.

8 servings

Calories per serving: 93   Fat: 1.9 g = 18% of total calories

RICE PUDDING

3 cups cooked brown rice
1 cup apple sauce
1 cup nonfat dry milk, dry form
½ cup raisins
⅓ cup honey
2 tsp grated orange peel
1 tsp vanilla
1 pinch cinnamon
3 egg whites, beaten stiffly
2 Tbsp pecan meal

In large mixing bowl, combine all ingredients, except egg whites and pecan meal. Fold in egg whites. Spray a 2-quart baking dish with cooking spray. Sprinkle with pecan meal. Spoon mixture in dish. Bake at 375° for 45 minutes. Serve with fresh or frozen raspberries. **6 servings**

Calories per serving: 208   Potassium: 445 mg
Fat: 1.8 g = 8% of total calories   Calcium: 162 mg

CHAPTER 17

DRINKS

SANS SOUCI FRUIT DRINK

2½ cups water
1½ cups frozen banana chunks
½ cup frozen raspberries
¼ almond extract

In electric blender, combine all ingredients. Blend until smooth. Serve immediately in tall glass garnished with a slice of fresh fruit and mint.   **5 servings**

Calories per serving: 89   Calcium: 11 mg
Fat: 0.37 g = 4% of total calories   Sodium: 5 mg
Potassium: 300 mg   Fiber: 3 g

LEMON WATER

The juice of 1 lemon added to four cups of water. I start every day, at home or at Sans Souci, with this refreshing drink. For variety you can add 1 cup of calcium-enriched fruit juices.
4 servings

Calories per serving: 4   Vitamin C: 8 mg

ALMOND MILK

14 whole almonds
2½ cups water
2 cups frozen banana chunks
Dash vanilla
Dash ground nutmeg

In electric blender, combine all ingredients except nutmeg. Blend until smooth. Pour into serving glasses. Top with nutmeg. Serve immediately.   **6 servings**

Calories per serving: 121
Protein: 2.8 g   Calcium: 30 mg
Fat: 5.6 g = 42% of total calories   Sodium: 5 mg
Potassium: 263 mg   Fiber: 2 g

PROTEIN DRINK

2 cups skim milk or soy milk
1 cup frozen raspberries
3 ice cubes
2 Tbsp soy milk powder
Barley malt to sweeten

In electric blender, combine all ingredients. Blend until smooth. Serve immediately.   **2 servings**

Calories per serving: 128
Fat: 0.82 g = 6% of total calories   Calcium: 317 mg
Cholesterol: 4 mg   Sodium: 127 mg
Potassium: 509 mg   Fiber: 4 g

RISE AND SHINE

3 cups water
Juice of 1 lemon
1 cup pineapple or raspberry juice

Combine water, lemon juice and pineapple juice. Serve in tall glass. Garnish with mint. At Sans Souci we start the day with this refreshing ambrosia. **5 servings**

Calories per serving: 17
Fat: 0.01 g = 1% of total calories
Potassium: 50 mg

Calcium: 7 mg
Sodium: 5 mg
Fiber: 0.06 g

PINA COLADA

¼ cup nonfat dry milk, dry form
1 cup water
6 ice cubes
½ cup pineapple chunks
1 capful each of rum, coconut and pineapple extract
Low calorie sweetener
6 oz pineapple juice

In electric blender, blend all ingredients except pineapple juice. Divide juice into 3 tall glasses. Pour blended mixture over juice for layered effect. **3 servings**

Calories per serving: 69
Fat: 1.9 g = 25% of total calories
Cholesterol: 0.31 mg
Potassium: 183 mg

Calcium: 36 mg
Sodium: 13 mg
Fiber: 0.41 g

CHAPTER 18

LETTING GO OF THAT
HEAVY BURDEN

Letting go of extra weight starts with your thoughts and priorities. Making healthy choices and acting on them brings you the most valuable gifts: good health and happiness. We all want to be happy, yet happiness is difficult, if not impossible, without health. Staying fit is not about effort and struggle; it can be a pleasure, not a burden. Treating yourself as a valued friend gets easier every day.

Here are some pointers to help you design a health plan to fit your specific needs and preferences

1. Make a lifelong commitment to a healthy lifestyle

2. Limit your fat intake to 18% of total calories

3. Walk 18 miles a week. Exercise is as important as eating properly

4. Include $18 \times 2 = 36$ grams of fiber a day

5. Tend to your emotional needs; 18 hugs a week feels good and is non-fattening

6. Plan a weekly menu, keeping in mind balance, variety and moderation

7. Prepare a food shopping list and stick to it - do not shop for food when you are tired or hungry

8. Store food out of sight and out of mind

9. Keep food as close to its natural state as possible: sun ripened "live, life-giving food"

10. Choose a variety of foods rich in complex carbohydrates and fiber, whole grains, legumes, vegetables and fruits

11. Eat small portions - overeating damages your health and your waistline

12. Eat only when you are hungry

13. Drink 8 glasses of water a day

14. Say NO to fat, sugar, salt, caffeine and alcohol

15. Eat most of your calories during the first half of the day

16. Meet your needs of love by reaching out to people instead of food

17. Ask for help and surround yourself with supportive people

18. Accept full responsibility and recognize your ability to take charge

Rejoice! You will be able to eat and enjoy food every single day of your life. There is no need to store it up, to overload in anticipation of famine.

YOUR BILL OF RIGHTS.

You have a birth right to

Receive and to give love

Enjoy eating without guilt

Live in a body that serves you well

Choose health

Choose happiness

YOU DESERVE TO TREAT YOURSELF RIGHT !

INDEX

SANS SOUCI SPA LIFE

Susanne Kircher opened Sans Souci Spa in 1980. This 80-acre country estate attracts guests from all over the U.S. and Canada. Sans Souci, French for care-free, offers a luxurious setting for weight control and life-style changes.

Sans Souci Spa blends European elegance and American know-how into an empowering approach to weight control, fitness, stress management and smoking cessation. A large part of Sans Souci's appeal comes from the individualized attention and personalized programs presented in a caring and nurturing environment.

Sans Souci has gained national recognition and is featured in nine Spa books and over 72 magazine and newspaper articles including *American Health, Shape, Vegetarian Times, Glamour, Exercise and Midwest Living.*

Our mission at Sans Souci is to empower you to improve your body, mind and spirit. We cultivate healthy life-style habits and give you the confidence to meet daily challenges with joy.

For information about Sans Souci Spa programs write or call:

Sans Souci Spa
3745 West Franklin Road
Bellbrook, OH 45305
Phone: 513-848-4851, or 513-435-9778

TO ORDER

MAIL ORDER TO: TRUDY KNOX, PUBLISHER
168 WILDWOOD DRIVE
GRANVILLE OH 43023-1073

	AMOUNT	FOR
Please send _____ copies of the book, *SANS SOUCI SPA DINING* $15.00 EACH COPY	$	books
ADD FOR POSTAGE. $2.00 for one or two books. Please add 50¢ for each additional book. For delivery outside the United States please add additional postage to cover costs.	$	postage
OHIO residents add 6% sales tax.	$	OHIO tax
Enclosed is ❑ check for or ❑ money order, **U S Funds only** for	$	**TOTAL**

Make check payable to: Trudy Knox, Publisher
168 WILDWOOD DRIVE
GRANVILLE, OH 43023-1073 .   U S Funds only, please.

Send *Sans Souci Spa Dining* **to:**

NAME: _____

ADDRESS: _____ APT #
SUITE #_____

CITY:_____ STATE: _____

PHONE: _____ ZIP: _____

PLEASE ALLOW 4-6 WEEKS DELIVERY TIME

QUANTITY DISCOUNTS
Trudy Knox, Publisher books are available at quantity discounts for educational, business or sales promotional use. For information, please write to Special Sales Department, Trudy Knox, Publisher, 168 Wildwood Drive, Granville, OH 43023-1073.